Revelation: Book of Torment, Book of Bliss

T&T CLARK STUDY GUIDES TO THE NEW TESTAMENT

Series Editor
Tat-siong Benny Liew, College of the Holy Cross, USA

T&T CLARK STUDY GUIDES TO THE OLD TESTAMENT

Revelation: Book of Torment, Book of Bliss

An Introduction and Study Guide

Stephen D. Moore

t&t clark

LONDON • NEW YORK • OXFORD • NEW DELHI • SYDNEY

T&T CLARK
Bloomsbury Publishing Plc
50 Bedford Square, London, WC1B 3DP, UK
1385 Broadway, New York, NY 10018, USA

BLOOMSBURY, T&T CLARK and the T&T Clark logo are
trademarks of Bloomsbury Publishing Plc

First published in Great Britain 2021

Cover design: Charlotte James

Library of Congress Cataloging-in-Publication Data
Names: Moore, Stephen D., 1954- author.
Title: Revelation : an introduction and study guide :
book of torment, book of bliss / Stephen D. Moore.
Description: London ; New York : T&T Clark, 2021. |
Series: T&T Clark's study guides to the New Testament |
Includes bibliographical references and index. |
Summary: "This study guide explores the relevance of the Book of Revelation, and the
continuing fascination that it creates for readers from both secular and faith backgrounds.
Stephen D. Moore highlights the transcultural effect that Revelation has not only on Christian
imaginings of the afterlife and depictions of Satan, but on every culture formed by Christianity,
forming a potent idea of what is to come in the world's eventual destruction. Moore introduces
all the key aspects of Revelation before offering a guide that considers what Revelation might
mean for our present, as opposed merely to the context of the text's creation, Moore turns to
empire-critical, postcolonial, feminist and ecological readings, arguing that all four themes
intertwine intricately in Revelation. In reflecting on the text's reception throughout the
centuries, with a culmination in its impact on 20th- and 21st-century US culture, the analysis
of the context of the book's initial creation, and applying the aforementioned contemporary
themes and tropes in a miniature commentary on the text, Moore writes for all those who are
drawn to this apocalyptic culmination to the Christian belief system"– Provided by publisher.
Identifiers: LCCN 2020036426 (print) | LCCN 2020036427 (ebook) |
ISBN 9780567696779 (pb) | ISBN 9780567696786 (hb) |
ISBN 9780567696793 (epub) | ISBN 9780567696816 (epdf)
Subjects: LCSH: Bible. Revelation–Criticism, interpretation, etc.
Classification: LCC BS2825.52 .M655 2021 (print) |
LCC BS2825.52 (ebook) | DDC 228/.061–dc23
LC record available at https://lccn.loc.gov/2020036426
LC ebook record available at https://lccn.loc.gov/2020036427

ISBN: HB: 978-0-5676-9678-6
         PB: 978-0-5676-9677-9
         ePDF: 978-0-5676-9681-6
         ePUB: 978-0-5676-9679-3

Typeset by Integra Software Services Pvt. Ltd.

To find out more about our authors and books visit www.bloomsbury.com
and sign up for our newsletters.

Contents

Acknowledgements

Thank you, Benny, for commissioning this volume for your series—and for waiting many more years for it than was reasonable. It must have seemed more than once that Jesus would return on the clouds before the manuscript appeared in your inbox. You exemplify the 'patient endurance' that the author of Revelation extols.

My Drew colleague Catherine Keller has been writing her own (more substantial) book on Revelation while I have been writing this one. Her mournful fascination with apocalyptic imaginings in our age of climate catastrophe and democratic disintegration has amplified my own.

I am also grateful to all the students/co-learners who read and debated Revelation with me over the years, not least the exceptionally invested members of my Revelation class at the Edna Mahan Correctional Facility for Women: Natalia Alvarez, Latonia Bellamy, Myrna Díaz, Jamie Farthing, Karla Freeman, Angie Sánchez, Ronda Slovin, Natasha White and Audrey Wilson. I dedicate this book to you.

1

Why read Revelation?

The book of Revelation is a glittering object, an extravagant concoction quite unlike any other book in the New Testament, or, indeed, the Bible, aside from Daniel – although it is really only Daniel 7–12 that rivals Revelation's relentless heaping of apocalyptic vision on apocalyptic vision. And what vivid, visceral visions Revelation piles up and piles on. They include:

- the surreal, imagination-straining, head-to-toe description of the risen Jesus (1.12-16), the only detailed physical description of Jesus, risen or not, in any New Testament text;
- the abrupt ascent to God's heavenly throne room (4.1-11) to allow the audience a front-row seat for the epochal scene about to unfold (5.1-7);
- the successive unleashing of the fearsome figures known as the Four Horsemen of the Apocalypse whose weapons are war, famine, pestilence and general mass slaughter (6.1-8);
- the systematic decimation of the natural world, ranging from such ecological horrors as 'all [the] green grass [being] burned up' (8.7) to the sea becoming 'like the blood of a corpse', causing every sea creature to perish (16.3, NRSV trans. here and throughout unless noted);
- the bizarre encounter between a woman 'clothed with the sun, with the moon under her feet', who also happens to be in labour, and a colossal seven-headed, ten-horned red dragon (12.1-17), Revelation's singular representation of the devil (contrast the altogether undescribed Satan of the four gospels and the Acts of the Apostles: we hear his voice on occasion [Mt. 4.3-9; Lk. 4.3-11], but he never erupts in the visual field of our imagination);
- the seven-headed, ten-horned leopard-like beast with bear's claws and a lion's mouth that emerges from the sea and is served by a second beast that rises up from the earth (Rev. 13.1-3, 11-12), further

examples of Revelation's hyperbolic villains (the villains of the other New Testament narratives pale by comparison);

- the beast-riding, blood-drinking woman labelled 'Babylon the great, mother of whores and of earth's abominations' (17.5) and her violent obliteration, first as a woman (17.16) and then as the city she has morphed into (18.1–19.3);
- the riding forth from heaven on a white horse of a celestial superwarrior who, although accompanied by the armies of heaven, has been appointed to defeat singlehandedly the sea beast, the kings of the earth and all their armies (19.11-21);
- the binding of Satan with a mighty chain and his consignment to a bottomless abyss for a thousand years (20.1-3);
- the consequent thousand-year reign of Christ on earth together with the slain martyrs, who are resurrected to rule with him (20.4-6);
- the Last Judgment and the casting of anyone whose name has not been recorded in the book of life into the lake of fire that burns with sulfur (20.11-15);
- the descent from heaven to earth of the holy city, the new Jerusalem, which turns out to be a colossal golden cube (21.2, 15-18);
- the climactic opening of a narrative window on the interior of the cube city, which is revealed to contain a recreated Garden of Eden where the redeemed will dwell forever (21.22-3; 22.1-5)

– to list only the more spectacular elements of Revelation's visionary deluge. But what does it all mean?

Revelation's reverberations

Needless to say, Revelation means many different things to many different people. The people whose views on Revelation mainly come to expression in the present book are critical scholars of the New Testament, that odd academic tribe most of whose members have one foot in the church and the other in the academy (like the angel of Rev. 10.1-3 who awkwardly straddles the land and the sea). Critical interpretation and interrogation of Revelation have had a relatively long history: their beginnings may be traced back to the eighteenth, or even the seventeenth, century (see Wainwright 2001: 63–5, 125ff.; Koester 2014: 53, 57). Critical readers of Revelation, however, have only ever represented a miniscule minority of those for whom the book has warranted serious attention. What motivates most people who become obsessed with Revelation is relatively straightforward: they read or hear the book as speaking urgently about the imminent future and as summoning them to prepare for that future in the present. It is harder to generalize about why critical New Testament scholars who teach courses on Revelation and/or write conference papers, articles or books on it deem it worthy of attention. I can only speak for myself.

I begin with a vignette. The affable undergraduate working summer hours in the school library, whom I will call Anna (I don't know her real name), has deduced from the ungodly pile of biblical studies books I'm checking out that I'm a 'Bible professor'. She has never taken a Bible course, she tells me, but thinks she probably should; what am I teaching this fall? 'The course I'm most looking forward to', I reply, 'is on the book of Revelation', whereupon her expression turns intense: 'That sounds amazing. I really believe we're in the end times as well.' That's the end of the exchange, as other library patrons are lining up behind me; but her words rattle in my head as I plod back to my office.

Anna's conviction that we're living in the end times is far from anomalous, at least in the United States. According to a relatively recent and frequently referenced Pew Research Center survey, 47 per cent of US Christians profess belief that Jesus Christ will definitely (27 per cent), or probably (20 per cent), return to earth by the year 2050, while only 10 per cent of US Christians feel confident that this will not happen (Pew Research Center 2013). Even among Americans who self-identify as religiously unaffiliated, 20 per cent believe that Jesus will definitely or probably return by 2050 (Pew Research Center 2010). Revelation is not the only New Testament text in which Jesus insists that his return is imminent ('I am coming soon'; 'See, I am coming like a thief!'; 'See, I am coming soon!'; 'Surely I am coming soon' – Rev. 3:11; 16:15; 22:7, 12, 20), but in the minds of millions it is the main such text.

What precisely Revelation says or does not say, however, about the Second Coming and the other 'last things' is almost beside the point. Relatively few of the more than 100 million US Christians who, according to the Pew survey, believe the end is definitely, or probably, at hand have derived that belief from personal study of Revelation or any other biblical text. Beliefs about Jesus' glorious return and other endtime events long ago ceased to be tidily contained behind church doors or within evangelical witness as traditionally conceived. Rather, such beliefs have infiltrated certain sectors of popular culture. They have been transmitted and disseminated through multiple media, and thereby taken root in many people who rarely or never read the Bible or hear it preached, a process we explore below in the latter stretches of Chapter 2.

Anna's assumption that I share her eschatological convictions – 'I really believe we're in the end times *as well*' – is entirely understandable. After all, here's a guy who not only reads Revelation but even teaches it and hauls cartloads of books on it out of the library as if to advertise his obsession with it. Surely, he must be convinced that Jesus is about to appear on the clouds any day. There certainly was a time when I did believe that, when I looked to the sky, both literally and metaphorically, both hopefully and anxiously, as did many other members of the end-times-attuned and Rapture-ready circles in which I moved as a young man. As much as anything, the present book obliquely tells the tale of why it is no longer possible for me to read or experience Revelation as I read and experienced it then.

But why do I continue to read Revelation at all – and not only read it but, as I have already confessed, teach it, and, as I'm doing here yet again, add my own scribblings to the seething ocean of ink that already laps on its shores? The reasons are many and also contradictory, as Revelation both attracts and repels me. I find Revelation to be an astonishing work of literature, a powerful work of poetry; the sinuous surreality of its imagery and the lyrical extravagance of its language never cease to seduce me, even while certain of its spectacles never fail to appal me. Another reason for my continuing fascination with Revelation is that to engage with it is to attach oneself to something vast and diffuse; for Revelation is more even than an immeasurably influential religious text, it is also a cultural icon – or, better, a transcultural icon – of the first order. It powerfully shapes the collective hopes and fears, not just of eschatologically oriented Christians, but of Christians in general.

In particular and down through the ages, Revelation has moulded Christian imaginings of the afterlife more than any other New Testament text. Revelation contains the only detailed descriptions of heaven in the New Testament (see esp. 4.1–5.14; 21.1–22.5; Luke comes a distant second in this regard: see 16.22-6; 20.34-6). Revelation also contains one of only two detailed New Testament descriptions of the Last Judgment, when the actions of every human being who has ever lived will be weighed and the doers consigned eternally either to heaven or to hell (Rev. 20.11-15; see also Mt. 25.31-46). Revelation's representation of hell, moreover, is the most graphic and horrific found in the New Testament. Those who refuse to worship Revelation's God and its Christ will be forced to

drink the wine of God's wrath, poured unmixed into the cup of his anger, and they will be tortured [*basanisthēsetai*] with fire and sulfur in the presence of the holy angels and in the presence of the Lamb [that is, Jesus]. And the smoke of their torture goes up for ever and ever. There is no rest day or night for [them].
(Rev. 14.9-11; see also 19.20; 20.10, 14-15; 21.8)

Hell in Revelation is 'the lake that burns with fire and sulfur' (21.8; see also 19.20; 20.10) and anyone 'whose name [is] not found written in the book of life' will be cast into it (20.15). 'Brimstone' is the archaic English term for sulfur; hence, 'to preach fire and brimstone' is to warn about the horrors of hell as Revelation represents them. (And the image of fire combined with sulfur is particularly horrific. In the ancient world, as David E. Aune notes, burning sulfur was used in siege warfare and was 'horribly effective because it stuck to the body' [1998a: 835].)

As indicated earlier, Satan also looms larger in Revelation than in any other New Testament text – literally, indeed, for Revelation's Satan is a 'great [or "massive": *megas*] red dragon' (12.3, 9; see also 2.9-10, 13, 24; 3.9; 12.4, 7-18; 13.2, 4; 16.13; 20.1-3, 7-10). Particularly significant is Rev. 12.7-12: the 'throwing down' of Satan from heaven to earth in this scene has traditionally been thought to be the tale of how Satan became what he is. Originally a glorious archangel named Lucifer (so the myth goes), Satan is here cast out of heaven for his sin of pride. This interpretation of Rev. 12.7-12 depends ultimately upon Isa. 14.12-15 as read through the lens provided by two extracanonical Jewish works, *2 Enoch* (see 29.3-4) and the *Life of Adam and Eve* (see 12–16). In the context of Revelation, however, Satan's fall is not a primordial event located at the dawn of time – so most scholars would argue – but an eschatological event (as in Lk. 10.17-18) scheduled for the end of time. Yet that has not prevented Rev. 12.7-12 down through the ages from powerfully shaping Christian construals of Satan's origins.

Revelation's influence, however, has not been restricted to the Christian imagination. Revelation furnishes not just self-identified Christians, but people in every culture formed by Christianity – even cultures now effectively post-Christian – with a repertoire of terms and images for representing the end of the world as we know it. Consider, for instance, the term Armageddon, which derives from Rev. 16.16 ('And they assembled them [for battle] at the place that in Hebrew is called Harmagedon') and is employed even in secular discourse as shorthand for world-annihilating nuclear conflict. For untold numbers of people, Christian or otherwise, Revelation is a potent instrument for thinking about 'what is to come' (cf. Rev. 1.1; 4.1; 22.6), whether personally or universally, and whether one has actually read Revelation or not. It functions as part of a transnational cultural unconscious that spans and blurs the religious and the secular.

Revelation, liberation, subjugation

So much for the future, what of the past and the present? Mainstream critical scholarship on Revelation is almost entirely preoccupied with the remote past, as we shall see: what John, the author of Revelation, writing within, and in response to, a specific sociohistorical context, intended to say in and through his cryptic book, and what his target audience, anonymous Christ-followers in the seven ancient churches to which his work is addressed (Rev. 1.4, 11), would likely have understood him to be saying. Most of the critical scholarship that has been published on Revelation during the past two centuries or more has been written in this mode, and, taken collectively, it constitutes an indispensable contribution to an adequate understanding of this ancient work.

A minority of critical scholars, however, mainly in the past thirty years, have not been content to remain solely in the remote past as they wrestle with Revelation. They also want to know what Revelation might mean for the present. Foremost among such scholars have been those who have read Revelation for liberation of one kind or another and found a powerful ally in the book's uncompromising critique of empire – easily the most scathing found within the New Testament – about which I shall have much to say below. These scholars have ranged from Allan A. Boesak, black South African anti-apartheid activist (Boesak 1987), and Pablo Richard, Chilean socialist and champion of the poor (Richard 1995, 2005), to – switching continents and contexts once again – David A. Sánchez and Jacqueline M. Hidalgo, both analysts of Revelation's reception in marginalized US Latinx communities (Sánchez 2008; Hidalgo 2016). With the latter two scholars, we have moved into the explicit realm of empire-critical and postcolonial studies of Revelation, another stream of work on this book that has also been flowing for some time (e.g., Howard-Brook and Gwyther 1999; Kim 1999; Ruiz 2003; Keller 2005: 35–94; Moore 2007, 2009; Nelavala 2009; Runions 2014).

In the classic liberationist tradition, epitomized by Latin American liberation theology, Revelation has generally been seen as surpassed only by the Gospel of Luke and the Letter of James as a New Testament resource for social justice. Relatedly, Revelation inspired many African slaves in antebellum America with hope for a better world, certain of its images being appropriated and transmitted through slave songs in particular; and that oppression-resistant stream of Revelation's reception history flows richly into contemporary African American biblical scholarship, most prominently in the work of Brian K. Blount (2001: 158–84, 2005a, 2005b, 2007; see also Martin 2005). Other scholars equally interested in liberation have foregrounded the oppressive elements that compromise Revelation's emancipatory elements, including other African American scholars (Smith 2014; Darden 2015).

Grave concerns about Revelation's representations of women, in particular, may be traced at least as far back as *The Woman's Bible*, the founding text of modern feminist biblical scholarship (Cady Stanton et al. 1895–8). Concerning Revelation's 'great whore … sitting on a scarlet beast' (17.1, 3) and its woman 'about to bear a child' and threatened by a dragon that intends to 'devour [it] as soon as it [is] born' (12.4), Elizabeth Cady Stanton, the work's principal author, wrote:

> The writers of the Bible are prone to make woman the standard for all kinds of abominations; and even motherhood, which should be held most sacred, is used to illustrate the most revolting crimes. What picture can be more horrible than the mother, in her hour of mortal agony, watched by the dragon with his seven heads and ten horns! Why so many different revising committees of bishops and clergymen should have retained this book as holy and inspiring to the ordinary reader, is a mystery.
>
> (1895–8: II, 184)

A century later, feminist critics of Revelation were still taking issue with its multifaceted misogyny (e.g., Keller 1996; Vander Stichele 2000), none more insistently than Tina Pippin (see esp. 1992, 1999, 2005). Still other feminist critics would take issue with Pippin's hypercritical appraisal of Revelation, arguing, in particular, that due weight must be given to the fact that its 'great whore' is a symbol for imperial Rome, and hence not an actual woman but an ancient city (see esp. Schüssler Fiorenza 1998: 205–36, 2007: 130–47).

Whatever stance one takes on Revelation's representation of women, there is no question but that its author provides a profusion of provocative material for interpreters interested not only in gender but also in sex and sexuality (see, e.g., Pippin and Clark 2006; Huber 2011; Moore 2014: 103–78; Menéndez-Antuña 2018). Measured in terms of the sheer quantity of text devoted to her (see esp. Revelation 17–18), Revelation's 'great whore' happens to be the second most prominent female character in the New Testament, eclipsed only by the mother of Jesus, and is, as the pejorative labels applied to her make plain ('whore' – 17.15-16; 'great whore' – 17.1; 19.2; 'mother of whores' – 17:5), a thoroughly sexualized character. Another of Revelation's female characters, the otherwise unnamed woman whom John contemptuously nicknames 'Jezebel' (on whom see Carter 2009; Lester 2018: 48–71), is also highly sexualized (see 2.19-24); and even Revelation's 'good' female characters, 'the woman clothed with the sun' (12.1-6, 13-17) and 'the bride' (19.7-9; 21.2, 9-10; 22.17), are represented in stereotypical ways that also invite searching feminist analysis (e.g., Pippin 2005: 134–7; Økland 2009). Revelation's protagonist, meanwhile, its Jesus, transgresses, or queers, the male/female binary distinction: when we first encounter him, he is (she is? they are?) described (in the Greek of 1.13) as having female breasts, as we shall see.

And then there's ecology (see, e.g., Meier 2002; Rossing 2002, 2005, 2020; Sintado 2015: 283–352; Kiel 2017), an ever more pressing preoccupation in New Testament studies, for reasons that hardly need belabouring. And just as with empire and sex/gender, Revelation is the New Testament book that, thematically speaking, devotes more explicit space than any other to matters we would now describe as ecological – not that Revelation could ever, for the most part, be mistaken for a green manifesto. Intrinsic to Revelation's plot is a relentless, divinely ordained destruction of the natural world (see esp. Revelation 8 and 16), culminating with that world's obliteration altogether and its replacement with a 'new heaven and a new earth' (21.1), one in which 'the sea [is] no more' (21.1; see Keller 2000) and whose centrepiece is an outsized city (see Martin 2009; Moore 2014: 235–43) containing an Edenic park (see Rossing 1999b; 2004: 141–58; Reid 2000) in which the redeemed are destined to dwell forever worshipping both God and a Jesus who now appears to have morphed permanently into a nonhuman animal, a lamb (21.2–22.5; see Moore 2014: 201–43) – further rich fodder for ecotheological reflection, as we shall see.

All of these overarching themes – empire, gender, sex, ecology – intertwine intricately in Revelation. For example, the Roman Empire is represented in Revelation as a depraved female prostitute whose sins are so unutterably abominable that they have fouled the entire earth, requiring that it be destroyed and replaced – but not before the 'great whore' has herself been slaughtered in a sexually sadistic manner. These and other less sensational themes and tropes are traced through Revelation in Chapter 4 below, which endeavours to provide a mini-commentary on the entire book. But first we shall, in Chapter 2, reflect on Revelation's remarkable reception through the ages, with special emphasis on its impact on twentieth- and twenty-first-century US culture; and we shall also, in Chapter 3, attempt to resituate Revelation in its original context of production: who wrote it, where, when, why and modelled on what?

2

Revelation's reception

Throughout the history of Christianity there has never been a time when individual Christians or groups of Christians were not convinced that they had succeeded in unlocking Revelation's code. We might be tempted to imagine that such imagined unlocking pertained exclusively to the impending end of the world, but the successive ages of the church yielded theological, christological, allegorical and even philosophical interpretations of Revelation, not to mention artistic and hymnic interpretations, in addition to dedicated eschatological interpretations. Of course, it is the latter line of interpretation that countless contemporary Christians, along with many non-Christians, immediately think of whenever Revelation is mentioned. It is an interpretation whose origins reach back to the second century and which has waxed and waned through the ages, boiling up intensely at times, subsiding to a low simmer at other times. Most high-temperature moments in the age-old history of Christian apocalypticism have been fuelled by the book of Revelation read in tandem with other biblical apocalyptic literature.

Any history, even a history of interpretation, is a selective exercise in exclusion as well as inclusion. The history of Revelation's reception told in brief below is the most visible one, the one that passes mainly through white European men. But other less visible histories might also be related, histories of how Revelation has been resistantly appropriated, or simply repudiated, by white women, for example, or how it has been resourcefully harnessed by African slaves and their descendants, or by other oppressed people. To these oft-submerged histories we will turn in due course, particularly in Chapter 4, our micro-commentary on Revelation.

How to read an apocalypse apocalyptically

The saga of Revelation's apocalyptic reception begins in earnest with the religious movement called the New Prophecy by its members, and, later, Montanism after its founder Montanus. It was a Christian apocalyptic sect that emerged in the mid- to late second century in Phrygia (what is now west-central Turkey) and flourished through the third century. Throughout Christian history, apocalyptic sects have most often been characterized by a conviction about *when* the end will occur – which year, even which day. But Montanism was characterized by a conviction about *where* the end would occur. The episode with which Revelation's climactic vision begins has 'the holy city, the new Jerusalem, coming down out of heaven from God, prepared as a bride adorned for her husband' (21.2). But it doesn't specify where precisely the heavenly city will land. The Montanists eagerly leaped into that gap, announcing that the New Jerusalem would alight on the elevated plateau stretching between the small, obscure town of Pepuza, which happened to be their headquarters, and another undistinguished settlement, Tymion, approximately 6 miles away (see Epiphanius, *Panarion* 48.14.1; Eusebius, *Church History* 5.18.2; Tabbernee and Lampe 2008: 102). Apocalyptic interpretation can be a particularly audacious appropriation of scripture, as this example illustrates, an attempt to make sacred history converge climactically on one's specific time and place, investing them, and consequently one's otherwise unremarkable existence, with ultimate significance.

Following the Christianization of the Roman Empire in the fourth and fifth centuries and the emergence of imperial Christianity, Montanism was largely stamped out. The next several centuries seem to have been notably devoid of widespread apocalyptic fervour. Much scholarly ink has been spilled on the question of whether or to what extent the approach of the year 1000 in medieval Europe was accompanied by a massive intensification of apocalyptic anticipation. Umberto Eco, in his contribution to a learned collection on the topic, ventures the following scenario. The book of Revelation, with its frightful Four Horsemen, in particular, riding forth to unleash war, famine and pestilence on the earth (6.1-8), would have seemed to tenth-century European Christians, both educated and unlearned alike, to be 'a chronicle of their present time. The opening of each seal must have appeared to an early medieval listener as the front page of the *New York Times* does to us.' But whereas most of us read or hear of mass-death or other disasters in the news and 'feel outside the stories they tell', great numbers of tenth-century hearers or readers 'felt themselves to be inside, within the world described by St. John' (Eco 2003: 126–7).

In contrast to the Montanists, such Christians did not need to forcibly funnel their lived daily reality through the book of Revelation, to the extent of renaming each of their villages of Pepuza and Tymion 'Jerusalem' as though to provide landing zone markers for the heavenly city when it finally began its descent (and thereby ensure that it would not land anywhere else). Rather, many tenth-century Christians seem to have experienced their lived daily reality as already contained within Revelation's visions, so deeply had the book's unsettling images saturated the culture. The book and the world had become one, an interwoven tapestry; and so one found oneself in the book whether or not one wanted to be there, independently of any forceful or inventive act of interpretation or any exceptional act of faith.

With the advent of the High Middle Ages, elaborate, often ingenious, attempts to relate Revelation to past, present and future history began to come into their own. Joachim of Fiore's *Exposition of the Apocalypse*, completed in the closing years of the twelfth century, was the most ambitious attempt of this sort yet to appear, reviving and intensifying a tradition that had been initiated by Irenaeus, Tertullian and a handful of other Church Fathers but had lapsed after the fourth century. Quite simply, Joachim's project was to cram into the capacious symbolic spaces of Revelation the entire sweep of Christian history from the first century down to his own time, and even beyond. How does Joachim manage this?

The multilayered intricacy of Joachim's interpretation cannot be captured here, but the following examples will relay the flavour of it. Revelation, as we shall see, is structured in terms of series of seven: seven letters to seven churches dictated by the risen Jesus; seven seals binding the mysterious heavenly scroll that has been entrusted to Jesus, now appearing as a slaughtered lamb; and so on. Joachim interprets the first of the seven letters, the letter to Ephesus (Rev. 2.1-7), as representing the age of the apostles, which he sees as having come to an end with the death of the apostle John. Essentially the same period of time is represented, for Joachim, by the breaking of the first seal and the unleashing of the rider on the white horse (6.1-2), and also by the blowing of the first trumpet (8.7) and the pouring out of the first bowl of God's wrath (16.2). Key overall for Joachim's code-breaking endeavour is an eschatological time period represented in Revelation as 1,260 days (12.6) or

42 months (11.2; 13.5; see also 12.14; Dan. 7.25; 12.7). The 1,260 days signify 1,260 years, for Joachim, which he understands to be the time between Christ's first coming (his birth) and his Second Coming. For Joachim, then (implicitly at least), Christ is destined to return in glory in the year 1260 (an interpretation Joachim's disciple Gerardo of Borgo San Donnino made explicit), and Joachim's interpretations of Revelation's sixth letter, sixth trumpet and sixth bowl take us up to that date, while his interpretations of the seventh letter, seventh trumpet and seventh bowl march us beyond it. With Christ now returned to earth and reigning over it, a golden age of the church will ensue, centred on two new monastic orders that will arise. For all intents and purposes, indeed, the world ruled over by the returned Christ will become, for Joachim, an enormous monastery – a 'monasticized utopia', as one scholar puts it (McGinn 2018: 9).

It is hardly coincidental that Joachim composed his commentary on Revelation while himself a monk and having lived most of his adult life within the confines of one monastery or another. Again and again, apocalyptic interpretations of Revelation have a habit of plummeting from the soaringly transcendent to wherever the interpreter happens to find himself or herself mired or immured, whether it be the village of Pepuza in the case of the Montanists, or Casamari Abbey in the case of Joachim, the monastery near Rome in which he first began to set forth his spiritual interpretation of Revelation. Indeed, this characteristic of apocalyptic interpretation accounts for much of its power and allure: its capacity to invest the ordinary, the humdrum, the mundane with epochal, world-transforming significance. Joachim might lay claim to being the foremost ancestor of the innumerable host of apocalyptic interpreters of Revelation, extending fully down to our own day, for whom the present – their present – is the moment towards which all human history has been tending.

From Revelation to revolution

What, in real-world terms, was at stake in the apocalyptic interpretations of Revelation that began to seep through the cultural fabric of Europe during the late Middle Ages? Not infrequently, issues of life and death were at stake. This is nowhere more evident than when we consider the catalytic role played by Revelation in the revolutionary apocalypticism of the Anabaptist movement in sixteenth-century Germany.

By now the Protestant Reformation had dawned. And the two pillars of Revelation interpretation had been, since the late twelfth century and Joachim's immensely influential *Exposition of the Apocalypse*: first, the conviction that Revelation is a prophetic and symbolic rendition of the entire history of the church from the age of the apostles to the end of the world; and, second, the identification the Antichrist as one or other pope (most often, the present pope) or the institution of the papacy itself. Martin Luther, the foremost Protestant Reformer, despite ambivalence about Revelation's evangelical value, would deploy both prongs of that established interpretation in his 1530 revision of his 'Preface to the Revelation of St. John' (see Luther 1960 [1530]) included in his German translation of the New Testament.

Meanwhile, apocalyptic convictions fed by Revelation, Daniel and other biblical books had been translated into social revolution by the radical reformers known as Anabaptists, preeminently Thomas Müntzer. Like many early Anabaptists, Müntzer identified the Christendom of his day with Revelation's Babylon (17.1–19.3) and hence as slated for spectacular divine destruction. Müntzer was also captivated by other punitive spectacles in Daniel especially, but also Revelation, that depict God humbling, even annihilating, the powerful (see esp. Müntzer 1993 [1524]: 98–114). But Müntzer was not content to wait passively on divine intervention to effect social transformation. His inflammatory preaching was a major catalyst for a mass peasant revolt in 1524–5 against the aristocracy and other elites. The revolt was mercilessly crushed, up to 100,000 peasants being slaughtered, and Müntzer himself was imprisoned, tortured and beheaded.

But the attempted translation of apocalyptic revelation into social revolution had only begun. Müntzer's disciple Hans Hut identified Müntzer and his fellow agitator Heinrich Pfeiffer as the two prophetic witnesses of Rev. 11.3-14, whose martyred corpses (see 11.7-8), like those of Müntzer and Pfeiffer, are left unburied by their enemies (see 11.9). Hut predicted that Christ would return in glory on Pentecost 1528 (the year before Hut himself would die horribly, as it happened) and set off on a missionary tour to recruit the 144,000 whom Revelation represents as Christ's elite followers (14.1-5; cf. 7.1-8). Undeterred by the grisly demise of Müntzer, Pfeiffer and Hut, yet another radical reformer, Melchior Hoffman, rescheduled the end of history to 1533, based on his own study of Revelation. Following Christ's glorious return (see Rev. 19.11-16) in that year, the German city of Strasbourg would become the New Jerusalem (see 21.2). When Jesus failed to appear in 1533, two of Hoffman's disciples declared that he had gotten not only the year but also the location wrong: it was Münster, not Strasbourg, that was destined to be revealed as the New Jerusalem.

All told, we have not strayed very far in our narrative from the town of Pepuza and the convictions of the second-century Montanists that it was destined to be the landing site for the New Jerusalem – although the intra-Christian wars that were consuming Europe by the sixteenth century had made the stakes of such convictions far bloodier. In light of the insurgent, sword-wielding turn Christian eschatology had taken, it is telling that the Anglican *Book of Common Prayer*, the first edition of which appeared in 1549, decreed that the books of the New Testament – with the sole exception of Revelation – be read through three times a year in Morning and Evening Prayer; or that Revelation did not feature in the readings for Sunday Mass specified in the Roman Catholic lectionary approved by Pope Pius V in 1570. Revelation was by then too closely associated with revolution in the minds of many ecclesiastical authorities.

After the mid-sixteenth century, however, the fires of revolutionary apocalypticism – 'activist apocalypticism', as one scholar aptly styles it (Riedl 2016: 262) – began to subside in Europe. Fervent, frequently elaborate interpretations of Revelation continued to be churned out in Protestant circles through the seventeenth and eighteenth centuries, most of them projecting the successive ages of Christian history onto Revelation's receptive pages, seizing on some set of recent or contemporary events as signs that the climactic events of history were imminent and routinely identifying the papacy with Revelation's beast from the bottomless abyss, its 'great whore', or both. But after Thomas Müntzer and his agitator associates and successors, there were no further peasant revolts stoked by apocalyptic preachers, and far fewer of the arch-apocalypticists themselves, even when they had the temerity to dub some reigning monarch or other pillar of the sociopolitical order the Antichrist, ended up in the torture chamber or on the executioner's block.

Revelation and Rapture

Some notable, and still influential, versions of 'quietist apocalypticism' (Riedl 2016: 270) – the kind that is content to wait on divine intervention, unaided by human force of arms, for the radical transformation of the world – had their origins in the nineteenth century, yielding a 'new futurism' (Wainwright

2001: 81). Instead of most of Revelation being seen as a veiled recital of church history from the age of the apostles down to the present age – that is, as principally prophesying past events – Revelation now came to be seen as principally prophesying events yet to occur in the world of the interpreter. In particular, John Nelson Darby's system for decoding Revelation (see Darby 1879–83, esp. V, 11, 28), which he developed in the 1820s and 1830s in conjunction with other evangelical members of the Anglo-Irish ruling class to which he belonged (see further Akenson 2018: 5, 40), became the foundation for a comprehensive apocalyptic construal of the book that was widely disseminated in the twentieth century, long after Darby's death, and continues to dominate Christian apocalyptic sensibilities in the present.

For Darby, Revelation's concern with its author's present context is confined to Revelation 1–3 – although certain of Darby's most influential dispensationalist successors, recycling an interpretation first proposed by Thomas Brightman in 1644, came to see Revelation 2–3 as a prophetic encapsulation of the entire span of church history, each of the seven letters to the seven churches symbolizing a different ecclesiastical age: the letter to the church at Ephesus (2.1-7) refers to the apostolic age; the letter to the church at Smyrna (2.8-11) refers to the age of persecution; and so on. With Revelation 4, we are launched into the future, for Darby, and remain there until the end of the book.

Two aspects in particular of Darby's interpretation of Revelation should be noted (neither of which originated with him, however, but were refined and popularized by him and his successors). First, Darby assigns the Jewish people a pivotal role in the eschatological timetable. He sees them represented in Revelation both in the 144,000 of 7.1-8 'sealed out of every tribe of the people of Israel' and in the sun-woman of 12.1-6, 13-17 whose 'crown of twelve stars' symbolizes the twelve tribes. The eschatological climax of history will not arrive until the Jewish people possess the entire land promised to them by God through Abraham (Gen. 15.18-20). This Darbyite conviction continues to exercise far-reaching influence even today. Filtered through the Christian Right in the United States, it has had a substantial impact on US foreign policy towards Israel since the late twentieth century.

Second, the Rapture was a towering concept for Darby and his disciples and continues to be for most contemporary Christians of an apocalyptic bent worldwide. The Rapture doctrine is not a single doctrine; it exists as a series of hotly contested variations. The most influential version, however, is the 'premillennial, pretribulationist' version enshrined in *The Scofield Reference Bible*, a Darbyite annotated study Bible published by Cyrus I. Scofield in

1909. By the end of the twentieth century, *The Scofield Reference Bible* had sold more than 10 million copies, becoming Oxford University Press's all-time bestseller in its more than 400-year history (Pietsch 2015: 174).

The principal points of Scofield's Darbyite doctrine were long ago distilled as follows by evangelical theologian Albertus Pieters (1998 [1938]: 15–16):

1 At any time there may take place the 'rapture', the sudden noiseless and invisible removal [the 'secret Rapture', as Darby himself termed it] from the world of all true Christians, to meet the Lord in the air [1 Thess. 4.17]. Simultaneously will take place the resurrection of all the redeemed who shall have died by that time, of all the past ages [1 Thess. 4.16]. Of all this the unbelieving world will hear nothing and see nothing, except that the people in question have disappeared.

2 This event will have such a remarkable effect that many hitherto unbelieving or only nominal Christians will turn to the Lord. These form the group called 'the tribulation saints'. They will begin to preach … the imminence of … the earthly rule of Christ ….

3 Immediately now appears the 'Beast' of Revelation [13.1-10], the Antichrist, who will bear rule both in church and state throughout the world.

4 Also about this time will take place the re-gathering of Israel …. To these, together with those we usually call 'the Jews', the land of Palestine will be restored ….

5 With these restored Israelites and Jews, the Antichrist will make a 'seven-year covenant' [Dan. 9.27] for the re-building of the temple in Jerusalem and the re-institution of the Levitical sacrifices.

6 In the midst of the said seven-year period, i.e., after three years and a half, the Antichrist will repudiate his promise and demand for himself divine worship [2 Thess. 2.4; Rev. 13.4, 8, 12, 15].

7 All the 'tribulation saints', and many faithful Jews not yet Christians, will refuse to render such blasphemous and idolatrous worship, and they will therefore be subject to a terrible persecution, called 'the Great Tribulation' [Rev. 7.14].

8 At the end of this period, all nations will come up against Jerusalem to battle – and will almost win [Rev. 20.7-9]. They will take part of the city; but a great earthquake shall cleave the Mount of Olives [Zech. 14.4] ….

9 This is the 'Battle of Armageddon' frequently referred to in the Scofield notes, although only once in the Scriptures [Rev. 16.16]. Christ will

come down at this point with a heavenly army, as in Revelation 19, and will overthrow the hostile forces. This appearance of Christ will be visible to the world, and is called 'the Revelation', in contrast with His coming seven years before, which is 'the Rapture'.

And so on through six more bullet points.

Two of Pieters's summative points are particularly worth noting. In his third point, Pieters, channelling Scofield and Darby, identifies the beast of Revelation as the Antichrist. That identification is both widespread and ancient; it may be traced back at least as far as Irenaeus's *Against Heresies* (5.28, 30), and thus to around 180 CE. Yet the term 'Antichrist' does not appear in Revelation itself. (Within the New Testament, *antichristos* occurs only in the Johannine letters: 1 Jn 2.18, 22; 4.3; 2 Jn 1.7.) Is there an Antichrist figure, at least, in Revelation, a character to whom that term might aptly be applied, and, if so, is that figure the beast?

Identification of Revelation's principal beast, the one who rises out of the sea (13.1), with the Antichrist is complicated by the fact that there is also a second beast in the book, the one who rises out of the earth (13.11). The sea beast is an integral component of the ancient Antichrist profile developed influentially and at length by Irenaeus (*Against Heresies* 5.25, 28-30) from elements lifted from 2 Thessalonians, Daniel and Revelation and creatively assembled. Irenaeus's sketch of the Antichrist begins with a declaration that the latter will usurp the worship properly due to God (*Against Heresies* 5.25.1). Irenaeus's immediate inspiration for this assertion is 2 Thess. 2.4; but Revelation's sea beast eventually becomes Irenaeus's principal source for his Antichrist portrait (*Against Heresies* 5.28.2; 5.30.1-4), and the sea beast is repeatedly represented as an object of worship in Revelation (13.4, 8, 12, 15; 14.9, 11; 16.2; 19.20; 20.4). Yet if the Antichrist is to be imagined as a distorted mirror reflection of Christ, as he so often has been, Revelation's land beast fits that profile at least as well as its sea beast. The land beast '[speaks] like a dragon', the dragon being Revelation's representation of Satan (12.9; 20.2), but the land beast also '[has] two horns like a lamb' (*eichen kerata duo homoia arniō* – 13.11), the lamb (*to arnion*) being Revelation's preeminent symbol for Jesus, as we have seen. In short, if the Antichrist is to be located in Revelation, he or it is distributed equally between two symbiotically related but ultimately distinct characters. Revelation's Antichrist is not one.

Secondly and more importantly with regard to Pieters's summation of Scofield's Darbyite doctrine, the scriptural reference I inserted for the Rapture event in Pieters's first numbered paragraph was not from Revelation but from 1 Thessalonians. Near the end of that letter, Paul and his co-authors Silvanus and Timothy (1.1) seek to reassure the Thessalonian church that their members who have died have not missed their chance for salvation even though Jesus has not yet returned. They write:

> For the Lord himself, with a cry of command, with the archangel's call and with the sound of God's trumpet, will descend from heaven, and the dead in Christ will rise first. Then we who are alive, who are left, will be caught up [Greek: *harpazo*; Latin: *rapio*, from which the term 'Rapture' derives] in the clouds together with them to meet the Lord in the air; and so we will be with the Lord forever.
>
> (4.16-17)

Without this Pauline passage there would be no Rapture doctrine. The passage provides the doctrine with its basic content: believers levitating into the air to meet the returning Jesus. Equipped with that image, however, Rapture proponents are able to read several other New Testament passages, including at least two in Revelation, as implicit or symbolic representations of the Rapture event. To Rev. 4.1, in which 'a door [is] opened in heaven' and John is told, 'Come up hither, and I will shew thee things which must be thereafter' (KJV), Scofield added the note: 'This call seems clearly to indicate the fulfilment of 1 Thess. iv.14-17. The word "church" does not again occur in Revelation' – after Revelation 2–3, Scofield means (although see 22.16 where the word occurs in the plural) (Scofield 1917 [1909]: 1334 n. 2). Scofield's implied assertion, in any case, is that the church is symbolically raptured in 4.1-2. The other such passage is Rev. 11.12. The two prophetic 'witnesses' (11.3) who have been slain by 'the beast [from] the bottomless pit' (11.7) are resurrected (11.11), after which 'they [hear] a great voice from heaven saying …, "Come up hither". And they ascended up to heaven in a cloud' (11.12, KJV). Proponents of the Rapture also routinely read this passage as referencing the event (although Scofield, apparently, did not).

Dispensationalism is the name for the theological and hermeneutical system that coalesced in the preaching and writings of Darby and his successors. Intrinsic to this system, and the reason for its name, is the notion that world history, from the Garden of Eden to the final events set forth in Revelation, is divided into a succession of divinely ordained 'dispensations' or periods, typically seven, beginning with the age of innocence prior to the sin of Adam and Eve. At present, we are nearing the end of the sixth dispensation, the age of the church (so the teaching typically goes), which will climax with the Rapture and the Great Tribulation and will be succeeded by the final dispensation, Christ's millennial or 1000-year reign on earth (see Rev. 20.4-6).

Darby, who was Anglo-Irish, as we saw, 'tried unsuccessfully to disseminate his views in the US during several missionary trips in the 1860s', as Paul D. Miller notes, adding: '[But] dispensationalism only became a mainstream phenomenon, with tens of millions of followers, in the twentieth century through two authors and one event' (2014: 12). That event was the founding of the modern state of Israel in 1948, a development that significantly boosted the credibility of the dispensationalists, because they had predicted it 'long before it was [imagined to be] remotely possible' (2014: 13). The two authors were Cyrus I. Scofield, whose dispensationalist reference Bible we have already discussed, and Hal Lindsey, whose slim, quick-read paperback *The Late Great Planet Earth* (1970) succeeded in funnelling into mainstream popular culture dispensationalist concepts such as the Rapture, along with more generic apocalyptic concepts such as the Antichrist, becoming the best-selling non-fiction book of the 1970s.

The book's jacket copy told its tale succinctly:

> The rebirth of Israel. The threat of war in the Middle East. An increase in natural catastrophes. The revival of Satanism and witchcraft. These and other signs, foreseen by prophets from Moses to Jesus, portend the coming of an antichrist ... of a war which will bring humanity to the brink of destruction ... and of incredible deliverance for a desperate, dying planet.

In its details, the book is a consummate product of US Cold War xenophobia, especially Sinophobia. Lindsey's take on Rev. 9.16, which numbers the demonic locust horde from the bottomless pit (9.1-3) as 200 million, is that it is a prophetic representation of a 200-million-strong Chinese army that will obliterate a third of the earth's population (in fulfilment of Rev. 9.18) by precipitating Armageddon (16.16) in the form of a nuclear holocaust (Lindsey 1970: 82, 84–7; the chapter is tellingly titled 'The Yellow Peril'). The Soviet Union, meanwhile, becomes another militarized apocalyptic horde, on Lindsey's reading (1970: 59–71), its ranks further swollen by the nations of Africa (1970: 68–9). Even Western Europe is demonized in Lindsey's eschatological script. He sees the early emergence of what will eventually become the European Union as a revived Roman Empire destined to be headed by the Antichrist (1970: 88–113). In *The Late Great Planet Earth*, Cold War paranoia balloons to apocalyptic proportions. But before the world is consumed in nuclear holocaust, true believers will be raptured out of it (1970: 135–45) and secured in the divine bunker.

Revelation in popular culture

What Hal Lindsey began – the updating and mainstreaming of classic dispensationalist concepts – Tim LaHaye and Jerry B. Jenkins completed. Unlike Lindsey, LaHaye and Jenkins are not content to issue yet another urgent warning that the Rapture, the Antichrist and the Great Tribulation are imminent. Instead, through the device of Rapture fiction, a preexisting subgenre of Christian fiction that they make uniquely their own, they plunge us into a world in which the Rapture is finally happening. *Left Behind: A Novel of the Earth's Last Days* (1995) opens inside the head of airline pilot Rayford Steele high above the Atlantic as he entertains titillating thoughts about 'drop-dead gorgeous' flight attendant Hattie (later to become personal assistant and sexual partner to the Antichrist, and as such the Whore of Babylon), while 'push[ing] from his mind thoughts of his family', especially his wife Irene, 'attractive and vivacious enough, even at forty', but somewhat 'repelle[nt]' of late due to 'her obsession with religion' (1995: 1–2). Within minutes, however, a panicked Hattie is reporting that dozens of passengers have vanished from the plane. 'Their shoes, their socks, their clothes, everything was left behind. These people are gone!' (1995: 17).

But this is only the beginning. The reader's lot is not to ascend to heaven with those who have been raptured worldwide, but rather to remain with those who have been left behind. A previously obscure Eastern European politician, Nicolae Jetty Carpathia, who is secretly the Antichrist, swiftly ascends in the chaos following the Rapture to become secretary-general of the United Nations (a demonized political body in *Left Behind* as in much dispensationalist culture). The inaugural *Left Behind* novel ends with the formation by Rayford Steele and his associates of the Tribulation Force, which, through most of the remaining novels in the sixteen-volume series, spearheads the resistance against the Antichrist and his minions.

Rapture fiction in the *Left Behind* mode reads like sacred science fiction (it is no accident that Netflix placed the 2014 *Left Behind* film in its 'Sci-Fi Movies' category), spiced with borrowings from the romance genre: square-jawed, take-charge male heroes and submissive female characters, the other defining trait of the latter being their physical attractiveness or lack thereof (see further Frykholm 2004: 90–1; Hungerford 2010: 127–8). Total sales for the series have been estimated as surpassing 80 million copies (experiencing a 60 per cent boost after 9/11 [Gribben 2009: 130]) – not counting sales for the forty-volume young adult spinoff series, *Left Behind: The Kids*. And there have also been *Left Behind* movies and a video game, as we shall see, in addition to graphic novels, a music album, a board game and adaptations in still other media.

With *Left Behind*, we are, of course, fully into the para-religious realm of Revelation and popular culture: specifically, a viral dissemination of themes and images from (or thought to be from) Revelation, through a medium that requires little or no actual reading of Revelation itself, and within a cultural milieu that requires no membership in any traditional church – or in any non-traditional church, for that matter. Millions of the *Left Behind* readership, indeed, do not identify as 'born again' (so Gribben 2009: 130).

Following the *Left Behind* phenomenon, the question of how many contemporary Christians hold beliefs that have been significantly shaped by dispensationalism has become even more perplexing – difficult, if not impossible, to answer with any confidence even for the United States, much less for the world at large. Certain beliefs that technically fall under the premillennial dispensationalist umbrella seem to function as 'default' or 'latent' articles of faith 'for many, if not most, Americans', as Amy Johnson Frykholm notes (2014: 443), above all those who think of themselves as evangelical, whether or not they would describe themselves as dispensationalist in addition. Barry Hankins observes: 'Almost all evangelicals today believe that Christ will literally return to earth someday, and most evangelicals are premillennialist, which means they believe that Christ will return before the inauguration of a millennial kingdom on Earth' (2008: 59) – precisely the sequence set forth in Revelation 19–20: Christ returns to earth, defeats his enemies and establishes his 1000-year reign, traditionally termed the 'millennium' (from Latin *mille*, 'thousand').

Fascination with Jesus' establishment of his millennial kingdom, however, extends all the way back to the earliest centuries of the church. What is particularly distinctive about premillennial dispensationalism is that it inserts the Rapture between the Second Coming and the millennium. But untold numbers of evangelicals (even using the term loosely), including many for whom the term 'dispensationalism' would elicit either a dismissive gesture or a look of bewilderment, also believe in the Rapture – and not necessarily because they heard it taught in Sunday school or preached from the pulpit. Since the mid-twentieth century, as Timothy Beal remarks, evangelicalism has been 'all about making Christianity popular, adopting cultural trends and new media technologies in order to appeal to as many people as possible' (2018: 179).

Iconic of early attempts in this regard were two that had the Rapture as their theme: the 1941 film *The Rapture* and, more especially because even more successful, the 1972 film *A Thief in the Night*. The opening scene of the latter has a young woman abruptly coming awake one morning as a sombre male radio voice reports from her bedside that millions of people worldwide have mysteriously disappeared during the night. 'Speculation is running high that some alien force from outside our system has declared war on our planet and some feel it to be a spectacular judgment of God.' Her terror mounting, the woman calls her husband's name, hurriedly following the sound of his electric shaver into the bathroom. The dropped shaver lies buzzing in the sink, its owner missing. The woman emits a shattering scream of the kind more often heard in horror movies. This is not accidental. As Beal has argued, *A Thief in the Night* was an important catalyst for 'the emergence of evangelical horror as a genre of film aimed at scaring people into conversion' (2018: 184).

In effect, the opening scene of *A Thief in the Night* is a dramatization of Lk. 17.34, which dispensationalists read as a further representation of the Rapture: 'I tell you, on that night there will be two in one bed; one will be taken and the other left.' The movie's title, meanwhile, alludes to several New Testament passages, including two from Revelation (3.3; 16.15), that represent the Second Coming as an event as unexpected as the stealthy nocturnal incursion of a thief or burglar (see also Mt. 24.43; Lk. 12.39; 1 Thess. 5.2, 4; 2 Pet. 3.10). The film's publicity poster proclaimed ' … and there will be no place to hide', implicitly a stern rejoinder to the desperate plea that the terrified inhabitants of the earth address to the mountains in Rev. 6.16-17: 'Fall on us and hide us from the face of the one seated on the throne and from the wrath of the Lamb; for the great day of his wrath has come, and who is able to stand?' (cf. Hos. 10.8; Lk. 23.30). The film's principal debt to Revelation, however, is its central deployment of the 'mark of the beast' motif from the book. In Revelation's dystopian vision, 'both small and great, both rich and poor, both free and slave [must] be marked on the right hand or the forehead' with 'the name of the beast or the number of its name', that number being, of course, 'six hundred sixty-six' (13.16-18; see also 14.9, 11; 16.2; 19.20; 20.4). In *A Thief in the Night*'s adaptation, a demonized United Nations (the United Nations being a stock villain in dispensationalist dramas, as noted earlier) ordains that none who refuse the mark of the beast, which takes the form of three rows of the digits 0110 imprinted on the forehead or hand, will be permitted to use money and may be subject to arrest and even execution.

Although a low-budget film (too low-budget even to feature a single levitating body), *A Thief in the Night* spread like wildfire through evangelical culture during the decades that followed its 1972 release, eventually being viewed by hundreds of millions and spawning three sequels: *A Distant Thunder* (1978), *Image of the Beast* (1981) and *The Prodigal Planet* (1983). With the more recent success of the *Left Behind* novels, the Rapture movie not only caught its second wind but underwent a genre transformation. With the *Left Behind* film trilogy – *Left Behind: The Movie* (2000), *Left Behind II: Tribulation Force* (2002) and *Left Behind III: World at War* (2005) – together with the 2014 *Left Behind* reboot starring Nicholas Cage – the genre shifted from Rapture horror to Rapture action thriller (Beal 2018: 192). So centrally does the plot now come to focus on the exciting exploits of the 'tribulation saints', the heroes of the resistance that pits itself against the Antichrist and his underlings in the wake of the Rapture that, as Beal remarks (2018: 193), one almost feels sorry for those who have been Raptured and are missing all the fun.

The same is even more true of the *Left Behind* video game, *Left Behind: Eternal Forces*, released in 2006, and with sequels following in rapid succession: *Left Behind: Tribulation Forces* (2008), *Left Behind 3: Rise of the Antichrist* (2010) and *Left Behind 4: World at War* (2011). The product description/marketing copy for *Left Behind: Eternal Forces*, which features single-player and multiplayer options, promises kick-ass, fist-pumping excitement on an apocalyptic scale. Potential purchasers are invited to:

- Wage an epic war of apocalyptic proportions in this real-time strategy game based upon the best-selling LEFT BEHIND book series created by Tim LaHaye and Jerry Jenkins.
- Join the ultimate fight of Good against Evil, commanding Tribulation Forces or the Global Community Peacekeepers, and uncover the truth about the worldwide disappearances!
- Conduct physical and spiritual warfare: using the power of prayer to strengthen your troops in combat and wield modern military weaponry throughout the game world.
- Control more than thirty units types – from Prayer Warrior and Hellraiser to Spies, Special Forces and Battle Tanks. Recover ancient scriptures and witness spectacular Angelic and Demonic activity as a direct consequence of your choices.
- Enjoy a robust single-player experience across an authentic depiction of New York City in Story Mode or play multiplayer games as Tribulation Force or the Antichrist's Global Community Peacekeepers with up to eight players via LAN or over the internet.

As the final bullet point indicates, the video game in its multiplayer mode boldly goes where Rapture movies or novels had not dared or thought to go, enabling the gamer to identify with the 'baddies' of the apocalyptic script, the Global Community Peacekeepers (the Global Community being what the United Nations mutates into post-Rapture) and their Satanic overlords, even to the extent of fighting for them against the forces of good. But even the forces of good in this game are ethically problematic, as numerous critics pointed out. The game imports directly from Revelation certain of its most troubling features, notably its convert-or-die theology laced with virulent misogyny (aspects of Revelation we will ponder in due course).

Other video games that mine Revelation for characters, imagery and plot lines (see Rosen 2013; Wagner 2015; Nicolet and Ischer 2019) do not even pretend to dwell within the evangelical fold. In *Gears of War*, for example, first released in 2006, humanity must do battle with the Locust Horde, an alien race patently modelled on the demon locusts of Revelation 9 who emerge from 'the bottomless pit', whose 'faces [are] like human faces' but with 'lions' teeth', who have 'scales like iron breastplates', powerful wings and 'tails like scorpions, with stingers' (9.1-11). The debt of *Darksiders*, first released in 2010, to Revelation is still more evident. Its hero, controlled by the game's player, is War, the second of the Four Horsemen of the Apocalypse: 'And out came another horse, bright red; its rider was permitted to take peace from the earth, so that people would slaughter one another; and he was given a great sword' (Rev. 6.4). War's principal opponents are two wicked angels; one of them is Abaddon, whom Revelation styles both king of the locust horde and 'angel of the bottomless pit' (9.11). By the end of the game, which is to say, by the time its final battle commences, Abaddon has morphed into the 'great dragon' of Revelation 12, and the player implicitly assumes the role of the archangel Michael in defeating it (Rev. 12.7-9; Wagner 2015: 13). If earlier we distinguished a horror genre from an action thriller genre in modern media appropriations of Revelation, it is clear that both genres have fused in video games like *Gears of War* and *Darksiders*. But I would contend that Revelation itself, when focused through a modern generic prism, is both horror and action thriller: most of the book moves with an action-infused speed that is positively breakneck relative to any of the other New Testament narratives (even the Acts of the Apostles) and most ancient narratives in general, and its horror credentials can hardly be questioned.

Biblical apocalypticism had, however, burst out of the evangelical corral long before the advent of Revelation-themed video games, most notably in a sector of popular culture that was anathema to evangelicalism because seen as infected by Satanism, namely, heavy metal music (see Till 2012; Moberg 2015: 53–66; Malkinson 2017). Images from Revelation already rear their gruesome heads in the lyrics of heavy metal progenitors Black Sabbath, but it is in Iron Maiden's 1982 anthem 'The Number of the Beast' that the Revelation-metal marriage is consummated. Nowhere in popular culture, moreover, is the fusion of Revelation and the cinematic horror genre so explicit – or so tongue-in-cheek cheesy – as in the music video for this song. The video opens with grainy black-and-white footage from the 1941 horror classic *The Wolf Man*, in which the eponymous werewolf, played by Lon Chaney, Jr., prowls through a foggy cemetery at midnight. Meanwhile, an overdubbed voice theatrically recites Rev. 12.12 and 13.18 (lightly modified) – 'Woe to you, o earth and the sea, for the devil sends the beast with wrath because he knows the time is short. Let him who hath understanding reckon the number of the beast, for it is a human number. Its number is six-hundred-and-sixty-six' – after which the song's first power chords come crashing in. The song's climactic verse seems to celebrate, not the Second Coming of Christ, but the coming of the beast/ Antichrist, who announces its impending return, threatens to possess the body of the listener and cause it to burn, and gleefully boasts: "I have the power to make my evil take its course."

The recurrence of Hollywood schlock-horror footage in the second half of the video ensures that the evil remains at the level of the laughable. Nevertheless, the release of the song and the album of the same name sparked much outrage in evangelical Christian circles in the United States, including public protests and ritual burnings of the album.

Revelation's next major metal moment came the following year, 1983, with the release of Metallica's first album *Kill 'Em All*, the longest track of which is 'The Four Horsemen', the most iconic example of the thrash metal subgenre the album is credited with popularizing. The track begins with a tremolo-picked, double-bass simulation of galloping horse hooves, after which it thunders at breakneck tempo through many verses of lyrics that announce the death-dealing arrival in "the dead of night" of the four apocalyptic horsemen of Rev. 6.1-8 and invite the listeners to ride with them or be mowed down by them. In effect, 'The Four Horsemen' song anticipates the Revelation-inspired video games we discussed earlier to the extent that it too invites or at least enables us to surf the cathartic wave of violence that surges out of John's ancient apocalypse and sweeps through its contemporary appropriations. But apocalyptic metal headbanging and video gaming also reprise, albeit in imaginary forms, the Revelation-fuelled, ultra-violent, would-be revolutions of early modern Europe, those fomented by Thomas Müntzer and his fellows. Unlike the radical reformers, 'The Four Horseman' had no alternative social structure to propose, nor did it have a beef with the Pope. In both its lyrics and its mode of delivery, however, it (too) represented a massive 'fuck you' finger poked in the eye of authority, most of all the evangelical Christian Right who valued Revelation for altogether different reasons.

All of this is but the tip of a pop-apocalyptic iceberg that extends through metal music of every genre and subgenre (down to the 2019 song 'Worship' by the pagan metal band Eluveitie; the song's lyrics, drawn from Revelation 13 and rendered yet more lurid, tell of the worship of the beast) and numerous other musical genres (a stunning, standout example being Johnny Cash's 'The Man Comes Around' from 2002, which again begins with a beast, or several: 'And I heard, as it were, the voice of thunder, one of the four beasts saying, "Come and see"') through films of every imaginable kind: good, bad or indifferent; religious, irreligious or irreverent; TV productions of many genres; comic books and graphic novels, Christian and otherwise; (other) children's books, board games, action figures, Lego sets and, as we saw, video games; and innumerable internet websites, many of them dazzling and alluring, many more of them dark and scary (see further Walliss and Quinby 2010; Howard 2011; Clanton 2012; Partridge 2012; O'Hear and O'Hear 2015: 235–83; Fletcher 2017).

What about politics? How do those for whom Revelation is, first and foremost, a book about the imminent future relate it to the political present? The immediate follow-up question, of course, is *which* political present? For the present has a persistent habit of slipping into the past. Emblematic of the challenge that the present presents for apocalyptic readers of Revelation is Hal Lindsey's attempt in *The Late Great Planet Earth* to ascribe eschatological significance to the expansion of the European Economic Community (EEC), which later became the European Union. Lindsey believes that the EEC 'and the trend toward unification of Europe may well be the beginning of the ten-nation confederacy predicated by Daniel and the Book of Revelation' (1970: 94), both of which contain visions of a beast with ten horns (Dan. 7.7; Rev. 13.1). When Lindsey wrote those words, the EEC contained six member nations. In 1973 that number expanded to nine and in 1981 to ten, at which point a crucial piece of Lindsey's eschatological jigsaw puzzle seemed to have slotted into place. But by 1986 the number of EEC member states had risen to thirteen, and at present the European Union (the EEC's successor) consists of twenty-eight states.

Undeterred by such disappointments, present- and future-oriented interpretations of Revelation have continued to stream forth. A conspicuous feature of such attempts has long been the almost reflexive impulse to identify major dictators, US presidents, or other prominent or infamous world leaders with the enigmatic beast of Revelation whose number is 666. Leading candidates for the beast in the modern era alone have included Napoleon Bonaparte, Adolf Hitler, Joseph Stalin and Saddam Hussein, to list only the dictators. Beast candidates have also included US presidents. In the past half century or more, indeed, to be an American president and *not* to be a beast-suspect in many evangelical Christian circles means only that one's presidency has been exceptionally bland and unremarkable. Gerald Ford, for example, seems never to have been a serious beast candidate. But Franklin D. Roosevelt, John F. Kennedy, Richard Nixon, Ronald Reagan, Bill Clinton and Barack Obama all have been (as has Hillary Clinton even without ascending to the presidency). What of Donald J. Trump?

As I write these words, Trump is still president of the United States. Even before he assumed the office, speculation erupted about Trump's possible identity as the beast of Revelation. Appropriately for a reality show president-elect, much of the speculation centred on the glittery details of Trump's celebrity lifestyle. Symptomatic, too, of the extent to which apocalyptic speculation has, in our post-postmodern moment, fused with popular culture at its most sensational and most ephemeral is the fact that what is probably the most widely read Trump-as-Antichrist exposé occurs not in an American evangelical tract (admittedly an endangered genre) but in a British tabloid newspaper, one better known for its topless models than its dispensationalist credentials. On 19 January 2017, the day before Trump's inauguration as the forty-fifth president of the United States, the *Daily Star* ran a story titled 'Is Trump REALLY the Antichrist? The Donald's Terrifying 666 Pattern Revealed' (Evans 2017). The article began:

> President-elect Trump [is about to] become the most powerful man in the world .... But internet boffins have been whipped into a frenzy over sensational claims he is Satan in a man's body. Conspiracy theorists believe that Trump is the 'biblically foretold harbinger of the apocalypse.' The evidence?
>
> One of Trump's buildings is at 666 Fifth Avenue – which he bought for $1.8 billion. And 18 = 3x6, so: 666. The Trump family is also in the process of building a $666 million tower at One Journal Square – with a reported height of 666 ft. They even claim that Trump Tower is satanic – as, again, it is reportedly 666 ft. high. Trump himself lives in 'gold-plated opulence' on the

66th floor. It doesn't stop there – because 2016 [the year Trump was elected] is considered by many to be 'the year from Hell'. And 2016 = 666 + 666 + 666 + 6 + 6 + 6.

Scared yet?

(Evans 2017: np)

Yes, a little. The effortless ease with which once esoteric apocalyptic lore has now been assimilated to tabloid culture *is* a little alarming, or at least jaw-dropping. The article refers us to a companion piece (Hickson 2017) from the same issue of the *Daily Star*: 'We have already seen how some see Trump as a time traveller who came from 2036 to warn of an ISIS nuclear war' (Evans 2017: np). Meanwhile, the 'related articles' column in Evans's piece includes one titled: 'Trump family become Pornhub sensation – but which person is EVERYONE searching for?' The teaser image is a photograph of Trump with wife Melania and daughter Ivanka, but Evans provides the clue by including in his own article an extensive slide show of Ivanka. Tabloid apocalypticism is spiced with sex and sexism, as we might expect – but so is Revelation itself, as we shall see. Evans's article also creates sources, even biblical sources, to support its claims, in good tabloid (some would say Trumpian) fashion, declaring of the Antichrist, for example: '"He will deceive the masses, and even the electorate" – Biblical prophecy.'

With its sexism, xenophobia and fictional facts, tabloid culture is an irresistible target for academics and other highly educated folk. But is this simply another way of saying that to scoff at tabloid culture is a reflexive classist gesture? Kevin Glynn cautions us: 'Typically, the most disparaged cultural objects are those consumed predominantly by the most devalued social groups' (2000: 4), in this case, working-class people. The tale of dispensationalism's dissemination throughout the social sphere – in recent decades, through the medium of popular culture – is simultaneously a tale of dispensationalism's descent down the social ladder. For dispensationalism began (or began in earnest, at any rate) in the highest echelons of British society, as noted earlier. It was in the vast Irish estate and palatial mansion of Viscountess Powerscourt in 1833 that John Nelson Darby, himself a member of an aristocratic family that included an Irish castle in its holdings, first publicly set forth his theory of a 'secret Rapture' to a rapt Lady Powerscourt and other members of the Anglo Irish elite (Akenson 2018: 40–1). To the degree that dispensationalism was, however incongruously, an alternative form of knowledge, a non-standard method for making sense of history and the world, it is perhaps not surprising that it should eventually trickle down to tabloid culture, itself the principal contemporary conduit for the circulation of unofficial and non-elite ways of knowing (for the latter, see Glynn 2000: 6–7).

And yet a niggling question persists: Hasn't every apocalyptic, present- and future-oriented interpretation of Revelation, from the second century down to its most recent manifestations (which, in the United States, would include the globally publicized prediction of dispensationalist radio personality Harold Camping that the Rapture would occur on 21 May 2011 and, when Jesus once more failed to appear, on 21 October 2011 instead), ultimately proved delusional as history has continued to rush on, unheeding of the faithful gathered on mountain tops to greet the returning Lord? And so a second question presses in behind the first: How else might Revelation be read?

3

Revelation's production

How we read Revelation depends on what we understand Revelation to be. The implicit assumption of any attempt to relate Revelation's visions directly to the present world – a world of unprecedented eco-crisis, abyssal income inequality, international terrorism and a 'war on terror' locked in a self-perpetuating spiral, an ever-proliferating parade of political autocrats (some of them democratically elected) and so on – is that Revelation's author beheld and recorded divinely bestowed visions whose meaning he himself could not possibly have understood. Such readers of Revelation might say with the apostle Paul, 'Now these things … were written down for our instruction, upon whom the end of the ages has come' (1 Cor. 10.11, RSV). How else might Revelation be construed? Critical scholars of Revelation operate out of a different assumption: John understood perfectly well what he was writing, and the Christian assemblies he was addressing, and among whom he exercised an itinerant prophetic ministry, would likely have understood it as well. Scholars consequently attempt to reconstruct the intended meaning of Revelation, verse by verse and section by section, in its original context of production and circulation.

What is Revelation?

The first critical issue to be considered in relation to the question 'What is – what was – Revelation?' is that of *genre*. A literary genre consists of an open-ended multiplicity of texts unified by similarities in structure, style or subject matter. 'Novel', 'play', 'poem', 'letter' and 'gospel' are all names of literary genres. In part, Revelation's genre is that of a letter, which in and of itself suggests it was originally addressed to specific recipients in specific circumstances. Revelation's opening and conclusion contain elements that were standard for ancient letters. Near the beginning of the work, the sender and recipients of the letter are identified: 'John to the seven churches that are in Asia' (1.4a; compare, for example, 1 Cor. 1.1-2; Jas 1.1; 1 Pet. 1.1-2). This is followed by a salutation or greeting, another typical feature of ancient letters. In Revelation, this salutation is Christianized – 'Grace to you and peace from him who is and who was and who is to come …, and from Jesus Christ, the faithful witness' (1.4b-5) – as it is in other New Testament letters (e.g., Rom. 1.7; Gal. 1.3-5; 2 Pet. 1.2). Revelation ends, as do other New Testament letters, with a benediction or blessing: 'The grace of the Lord Jesus be with all the saints. Amen' (Rev. 22.21; compare, for example, 2 Cor. 13.14; Eph. 6.23-4; Jude 24-5).

If Revelation is a letter in terms of genre, it is also, and more importantly, an apocalypse. The term 'apocalypse' derives from *apokalypsis*, the first word of Revelation in Greek, a noun that, depending on its context, means 'uncovering', 'unveiling', 'disclosure', 'manifestation' or 'revelation': '[The] revelation of Jesus Christ [*Apokalypsis Iēsou Christou*], which God gave him to show his servants … ' (1.1; the word is particularly common in the Pauline letters: see, for example, Rom. 16.25; 1 Cor. 1.7; 2 Cor. 12.1, 7; Gal. 1.12; 2.2; Eph. 3.3; 2 Thess. 1.7). The book derives its title, then, from its opening word; but John is not using *apokalypsis* (which can also be translated 'apocalypse', and so the book is also known as the Apocalypse of John, or, simply, the Apocalypse) as a genre term. It was only later that 'apocalypse' came to be used explicitly as the name of a distinctive literary genre. How much later is hard to say. By the late second or early third century, we find Clement of Alexandria applying the word 'apocalypse' in genre-like fashion to a visionary work attributed to the apostle Peter (Clement of Alexandria, *Selections from the Prophetic Scriptures* 41.2; 48.1; 49:1), while the document variously known as the Muratorian Fragment or the Muratorian Canon, probably composed in the fourth century, speaks of 'the apocalypses of John and Peter' (line 71). It is only in the early nineteenth century, however, that the word 'apocalypse' begins to crystallize fully as the technical term for an ancient literary genre.

Specifically, the genre of apocalypse, as conceived by most biblical scholars, encompasses ancient Jewish and Christian works that purport to reveal divine secrets, especially (although not exclusively) eschatological secrets. Daniel and Revelation, the two biblical books that are deemed to be full-fledged examples of the apocalyptic genre, are members of a much larger literary family (as the very term 'genre' indeed implies). Several dozen works at minimum constitute this family (see the articles in Collins 1979 for details), and so it is an extrabiblical genre for the most part. Revelation appears to have been the earliest Christian apocalypse. Other early Christian apocalypses, such as the *Apocalypse of Peter*, the *Shepherd of Hermas* and the *Apocalypse of Paul*, are dated significantly later than Revelation. Certain Jewish apocalypses, however, are dated earlier than, or roughly contemporary with, Revelation. As such, they are highly relevant for contextualizing the literary genre to which Revelation belongs.

The most extensive of the ancient Jewish apocalypses is the *First Book of Enoch*, a colossal compendium of esoteric lore. More precisely, *1 Enoch* is an anthology of five apocalyptic books composed between the third century BCE and the first century CE. Like almost all ancient Jewish or Christian apocalypses (Revelation and the *Shepherd of Hermas* appear to be the only exceptions, as we shall see), *1 Enoch* is pseudonymous – that is to say, fictitiously written in the name of a revered figure from the past. Enoch, who appears briefly and enigmatically in the Hebrew Bible (Gen. 5.21-4; see also 4.17-18; 5.18-19; 1 Chron. 1.3), is the first-person speaker in this apocalypse: 'Enoch … saw the vision of the Holy One in the heavens, which the angels showed me, and from them I heard everything' (*1 Enoch* 1.2; quotations from *1 Enoch* throughout are from Charlesworth 2010). Further visions of Enoch are related in the *Second Book of Enoch*, which may date from the first century CE, and the *Third Book of Enoch*, which appears to be much later.

Other ancient Jewish apocalypses purport to be the visions of more obvious luminaries, heroes of salvation history, such as Abraham or Ezra, or more obscure figures associated with such luminaries, notably Baruch, secretary to the prophet Jeremiah (see Jer. 36.4, 17-18, 26), who also has three books attributed to him. The *Fourth Book of Ezra* and the *Second Book of Baruch*, both commonly dated to the end of the first century CE, are of particular interest to scholars of ancient apocalyptic literature, and not only because of their relative antiquity. Like Daniel 7–12, *1 Enoch* (the earliest material of which appears to pre-date Daniel), *2 Enoch* and Revelation, *4 Ezra* and *2 Baruch* contain certain (even if not all) of the classic elements of the apocalyptic genre, making them further exemplars of the genre. Such elements include:

- otherworldly journeys in which the visionary is miraculously transported to heaven and/or the abode of the dead and shown what they contain (*1 Enoch* 1–36, called the Book of the Watchers, is the classic early example of this device; it also occurs in Revelation, as we shall see);

- visions involving bizarre symbolic creatures, often as characters in dramatic retellings of the rise and fall of empires and other historical events, mainly presented as prophecies of things to come (Daniel 7–12 is the paradigmatic early example of this device; symbolic creatures also abound in Revelation, and veiled historical recitals also feature in it, as we shall also see);
- and explanations of such visions provided by an angelic interpreter or some other supernatural authority (a device already found in Ezekiel 40–48 and Zechariah 1–6, but particularly prominent in *1 Enoch* and *4 Ezra*; in Revelation it is most evident in 7.13-17 and 17.1-18).

Profound family resemblances exist, then, between Revelation and certain of the ancient Jewish apocalypses. As an example, consider two descriptions of otherworldly journeys, the first from *1 Enoch* and the second from Revelation. Enoch has a vision, 'and in the vision, the winds were causing me to fly and rushing me high up into heaven' (*1 Enoch* 14.8). Arriving in heaven, Enoch finds himself in a throne room:

> And I observed and saw … a lofty throne – its appearance was like crystal and its wheels [cf. Ezek. 1.15-16] like the shining sun; and [I heard?] the voice of the cherubim; and from beneath the throne were issuing streams of flaming fire. It was difficult to look at it. And the Great Glory was sitting upon it – as for his gown, which was shining more brightly than the sun, it was whiter than any snow. None of the angels was able to come in and see the face of the Excellent and the Glorious One; and no one of the flesh can see him – the flaming fire was round about him, and a great fire stood before him. No one could come near unto him from among those that surrounded the tens of millions [that stood] before him.
>
> (14.18-22)

Revelation 4.1-6 presents a scene strikingly similar to *1 Enoch* 14.8, 18-22, also involving the visionary's ascent to heaven and an elaborate description of a heavenly throne room and a numinous figure seated on the throne who is so glorious as to beggar description. A little later we learn that, just as in Enoch's vision, 'many angels' surround the divine throne in Revelation. They number 'myriads of myriads and thousands of thousands' (Rev. 5.11).

These visions of God in *1 Enoch* and Revelation are intimately related in turn to Dan. 7.9-10, which narrates yet another heavenly throne room scene. Fire also surrounds the throne in Daniel's apocalyptic vision, and the awesome being seated on the throne is also attended by innumerable angelic courtiers. Moreover, Revelation's heavenly throne room scene is only one of many elements in Revelation that find close parallels in other ancient apocalypses. John of Revelation recycles extensively images, phrases and motifs from the book of Daniel (see Beale 2010), and he may also be channelling *1 Enoch* on occasion (compare, for example, *1 Enoch* 9.4, 'And they said to their Lord, the King: "Lord of Lords, God of Gods, King of Kings!"', with Rev. 19.16, 'On his robe and on his thigh he has a name inscribed, "King of kings and Lord of lords"'). Beyond such localized borrowings, however, John is able to write the particular book he writes only because he has internalized an intricate but unwritten set of rules for generating apocalyptic discourse.

In consequence of such considerations, although Revelation presents itself throughout as a vision report – 'Write in a book what you see' (1.10-11; see also 1.19; 2.1, 8, 12, 18; 3.1, 7, 14; 10.4; 14.13; 19.9; 21.5) – many critical scholars read Revelation instead as a literary creation. (To cite but one example of this common critical assumption, it appears to pervade David E. Aune's colossal commentary on Revelation [1997, 1998a, 1998b] without ever being explicitly named.) In other words, such scholars believe Revelation was composed, not in response to a series of visions vouchsafed to its author, but rather in accordance with the literary conventions of the ancient apocalyptic genre, one such convention being the vision report. Other scholars, however, most of all those on the evangelical end of the critical spectrum, do not feel obliged to pronounce Revelation either a 'vision report' or a 'literary creation', seeing these alternatives as a false dichotomy. Their assumption is rather that the author of Revelation indeed had a visionary experience and had recourse to the conventions of the apocalyptic genre to commit it to writing. (This assumption seems to inform, from start to finish, for example, G. K. Beale's equally massive commentary on Revelation [1999].)

Understanding Revelation as an apocalypse, however, only takes us so far in making sense of this richly layered text. It does not account for many of Revelation's details. When one grapples with Revelation at the sentence level, one soon discovers that the majority of its images are drawn from Jewish Scripture, most especially from the books of Isaiah, Ezekiel, Daniel and Psalms, although also from as many as twenty other books. Indeed, Revelation contains more allusions to Jewish Scripture (both the Hebrew Bible and its ancient Greek translations) than any other New Testament text. Revelation contains no formal quotations of scripture, however, of the kind found in the other New Testament narratives (e.g., Mt. 4.13-16; Mk 1.2-3; Jn 12.38-40; Acts 2.16-21). Instead, the very fabric of Revelation is, for the most part, composed of a dense tissue of scriptural allusions, with half-dozen or more scriptural passages often coalescing in a single image or brief scene.

Moreover, images drawn from Jewish Scripture regularly balloon in Revelation, expanding from the mundane to the cosmic, or at least the colossal. Consider, for example, the transformation of Jer. 51.59-64 into Rev. 18.21. In the former episode, the prophet Jeremiah commands his accomplice Seraiah to cast into the middle of the river Euphrates, where it flows through the city of Babylon, a stone to which is tied a scroll containing Jeremiah's oracles against Babylon and to pronounce the following curse as he does so: 'Thus shall Babylon sink, to rise no more, because of the disasters that I [the God of Israel] am bringing on her.' In Revelation's redesign of the scene, Seraiah's modest stone, presumably of a size capable of being cast into the middle of a wide river, becomes 'a stone like a great millstone'; the river itself becomes a sea; and Seraiah is replaced by 'a mighty angel' who, however, when he casts the massive stone into the sea utters essentially the same oracle against Babylon (now a cipher for Rome) as his predecessor did: 'With such violence Babylon the great city will be thrown down, and will be found no more.' The most sustained example of Revelation's apocalyptic magnification of traditional material, as we shall see, is its transformation of the plagues inflicted by Moses on the land of Egypt in the book of Exodus (7.1–15.21) into cosmic disasters that afflict not only colossal areas of the earth and sea but the heavenly bodies in addition (Rev. 8.6–9.21; 11.15-19; 16.1-21). Apocalypse in the register exemplified by Revelation regularly amounts to Jewish scripture being recycled through a hyperbolic amplifier.

What's in a number?

In Revelation's opening vision, John is instructed by the risen Jesus to write seven letters to seven churches in the Roman province of Asia (1.10-11; see also 1.4a), the westernmost province of the larger geographical region known (somewhat confusingly) as Asia Minor that extended from the Aegean to the western Euphrates, thus corresponding roughly to modern Turkey. The number seven looms large in Revelation, as we are about to see, but not just in Revelation. Seven was a highly significant, sometimes sacred number in many ancient cultures. In ancient Egypt, for instance, seven symbolized perfection and totality, or cosmic order more generally. Similar significance was ascribed to seven in ancient Babylon, Persia and Greece, and, through (further) cultural osmosis, in ancient Israel (look no further than the seven-day schema of the first Genesis creation account,

1.1–2.4a) and early Judaism in addition. For example, the number seven is accorded weighty theological significance in the writings of the ancient Jewish philosopher Philo of Alexandria (to whom we shall return), as well as in the apocalyptic writings that make up the *First Book of Enoch*. Seven also features prominently and symbolically in the Gospel of John, which structures Jesus' public activity around seven 'signs' (*sēmeia*) or miracles (2.1-11; 4.46-53; 5.1-9; 6.1-15; 6.16-21; 9.1-41; 11.1-44), attributes to him seven solemn pronouncements beginning with the divine words 'I am' (6.35; 8.12; 10.7, 11; 11.25; 14.6; 15.1; cf. Exod. 3.14) and so on. But if the author of John's Gospel is preoccupied by the number seven, the author of Revelation is obsessed with it, exhibiting more reverence for it than any of his apocalyptic predecessors or contemporaries.

First and most obviously, Revelation is structured around major series of seven. The first such series is, as we have seen, the seven letters that the risen Jesus is depicted as dictating to seven *ekklēsiai* ('assemblies', 'churches') situated in seven cities (Ephesus, Smyrna, Pergamum, Thyatira, Sardis, Philadelphia and Laodicea) in the Roman province of Asia (Rev. 1.9–3.22). John represents Revelation as a prophecy (22.7, 10, 18-19), one intended to be read aloud in the churches (1.3; cf. Col. 4.16; 1 Thess. 5.26-7), and himself as a prophet (Rev. 10.11), perhaps even a member of a prophetic 'brotherhood' (see 22.9, 'you and your brothers the prophets [*tōn adelphōn sou tōn prophētōn*]', together with 22.16, 'I, Jesus, sent my angel to you [plural: *hymin*] with this testimony for the churches'; see also 19.10; 22.6). Was John's prophetic activity confined to, or centred on, the seven cities named in Revelation 1–3? Did they constitute his circuit for an itinerant prophetic ministry? Or do these seven churches stand symbolically for the entire church of Roman Asia as a whole (recall that seven was the number of totality), or even for the entire church of John's day throughout the Roman Empire and beyond? These latter possibilities are probably unlikely. In the seven letters to the seven churches, John has very specific, locally situated things to say to each of them through his numinous mouthpiece, the 'one like a Son of Man'. Still, even if John was active in Asian churches beyond those named in Revelation (e.g., those of Hieropolis or Colossae, both geographically adjacent to Laodicea, the three in combination often referred to by archaeologists as the tri-cities of the Lycus Valley), he may have limited the letters to seven in order to elevate that number to prominence.

The second explicit, plot-propelling series of seven in Revelation begins in 6.1. Jesus has made another dramatic appearance in the narrative, this time as 'a Lamb standing as if it had been slaughtered' (5.6, a pivotal scene to which we shall return) and has been entrusted with a mysterious scroll 'sealed with seven seals' (5.1). Seals of wax, soft clay or lead are what ancient audiences would have been predisposed to imagine here (Koester 2014: 374). When the Lamb breaks each of the first six seals, eschatological events, mainly of a catastrophic nature, unfold or are foretold (6.1–7.17). What scholars have tended to call an 'interlude' or 'digression' (7.1-17) – the first of three in the book – precedes the opening of the seventh seal (8.1). The latter event ('When the Lamb opened the seventh seal, there was silence in heaven for about half an hour') appears to be an intentional, suspense-generating anticlimax. It does not precipitate the end of history, but merely initiates another major series of seven (the third such series, following the seven letters and the seven seals). Seven angels are supplied with seven trumpets, and each proceeds to blow his trumpet in turn. As each trumpet is blown, further calamities are unleashed on the earth and its inhabitants (8.6–11.18).

Just as an 'interlude' separated the opening of the sixth and seventh seals, so now an interlude separates the blowing of the sixth and seventh trumpets (10.1–11.14). The narrative suspense is further heightened by the announcement of yet another angel, the most spectacular in this angel-thronged book: he is 'wrapped in a cloud, with a rainbow over his head'; his face is 'like the sun' and his legs 'like pillars of fire'; he stands with one foot 'on the sea' and the other 'on the land'; and his voice is 'like a lion roaring' (10.1-3). He proceeds to swear that when the seventh trumpet is blown, 'the mystery of God will be fulfilled' (10.6-7). Then John is readied anew for the task of prophecy (10.11). Like the prophet Ezekiel before him, he is given a scroll to eat (Ezek. 2.8–3.3; Rev. 10.8-10). God has put his words in the prophet's mouth – literally.

Finally, the seventh trumpet is blown (11.15). 'God's temple in heaven' is opened as a result (11.19). At first blush, this does not quite seem the fulfilment of 'the mystery of God' that the mighty angel swore would follow the blowing of the seventh trumpet (10.7). The eschatological significance of the opening of the heavenly temple is not revealed until 15.5-8. In the meanwhile, we encounter Revelation's longest and most important 'interlude', 12.1–14.20, in which the woman clothed with the sun, the great red dragon, the sea beast and the land beast are all introduced. In 15.1-8, we are returned to the heavenly temple, now opened as a result of the seventh trumpet being blown (11.15, 19). Seven angels process out of the temple bearing 'seven golden bowls full of the wrath of God' (11.7). These seven angels proceed, one by one, to pour the contents of the bowls out upon the earth and its remaining inhabitants, again with horrific consequences (16.1-21).

Revelation's fourfold series of seven – letters, seals, trumpets, bowls – provides the bones of a structure for the book, other sections lining up in relation to it:

The Prologue (1.1-8)
The Vision of the Son of Man (1.9-20)
The Seven Letters to the Seven Churches (2.1–3.22)
The First Six Seals (4.1–6.17)
The First Interlude (7.1-17)
The Seventh Seal and the First Six Trumpets (8.1–9.21)
The Second Interlude (10.1–11.14)
The Seventh Trumpet and the Third Interlude (11.15–14.20)
The Seven Bowls (15.1–16.21)
The Fall of Babylon (17.1–19.10)
The Final Battles and the Last Judgment (19.11–20.15)
The New Jerusalem (21.1–22.5)
The Epilogue (22.6-21)

Some scholars have argued that in addition to the four major explicit, or numbered, series of seven, there are in Revelation two major unnumbered series of seven, the first of them distributed mainly through 12.1–15.1 and the second found in 19.11–21.8 (or 22.5); but most have not found the case for these additional major series of seven convincing (see further Yarbro Collins 2001: 13–16).

Commanding wider acceptance are claims that Revelation, in addition to being structured around four major series of seven, is also studded with minor series of seven. For instance, the blessing with which Revelation opens ('Blessed is the one who reads aloud the words of the prophecy'–1.3) is only the first of seven such blessings that punctuate the narrative (see also 14.13; 16.15; 19.9; 20.6; 22.7, 14). The title Christ (*Christos*) also occurs seven times in the book (1.1, 2, 5; 11.15; 12.10; 20.4, 6), and the bearer of that title, Jesus, announces seven times that he is 'coming' (*erchomai*) – that is, returning in glory (2.5, 16; 3.11; 16.15; 22.7, 12, 20).

Multiples of seven also feature in Revelation. The name Jesus (*Iēsous*) occurs fourteen times, seven of these occurrences in the phrase 'the witnesses of Jesus' (*hoi martyres Iēsou*–1.1, 2, 5, 9 [twice]; 12.17; 14.12; 17.6; 19.10 [twice]; 20.4; 22.16, 20, 21). The term 'Spirit' (*pneuma*), in the sense of 'Holy Spirit', also occurs fourteen times (1.10; 2.7, 11, 17, 29; 3.6, 13, 22; 4.2; 14.13; 17.3; 19.10; 21.10; 22.17), while the title Lamb (*arnion*), the most important christological title in Revelation, is applied to Jesus twenty-eight times (5.6, 8, 12, 13; 6.1, 16; 7.9, 10, 14, 17; 8.1; 12.11; 13.8; 14.1; etc.).

The author of Revelation could hardly have expected his target audiences, who would not have had opportunity to pore over the details of the written text in the manner of modern scholars but would rather have heard it read aloud or performed in their assemblies (see 1.3; 22.18), to discern the minor series of seven and multiples of seven that he meticulously threaded through his narrative. The function of these subtle numerical patterns may rather have been that of imparting a mystical, magical or talismanic quality to his book (cf. Thomas 2010: 127). John's book would then mirror his conception of the world and its history, John embedding in the book certain of the hidden numerical designs he believes God has embedded in the world as it moves towards the consummation of its history.

Not all the instances of seven in Revelation occur in series, whether evident or concealed. The number also features prominently in physical descriptions of the book's warring characters. The 'great red dragon', explicitly identified as Satan (12.3, 9; 20.2), has seven heads, as does the dragon's primary agent, the 'beast [that] ris[es] out of the sea' (13.1; 17.3, 7, 9). Revelation's sea beast is a composite of the 'four great beasts' that Daniel sees '[coming] up out of the sea' in his own vision, and those four beasts together, as it happens, possess a total of seven heads (Dan. 7.1-7). Meanwhile, the Lamb, who is the crucified and resurrected Jesus and the principal opponent of the dragon and the sea beast, itself possesses, not seven heads, but rather 'seven horns and seven eyes, which are the seven spirits of God sent out into all the earth' (Rev. 5.6). The earth-roving seven spirits are, in turn, it would seem, a metaphor for God's omniscience lifted from the book of Zechariah (4.10b), while the Lamb's seven horns may be read as a metaphor for God's omnipotence (see, e.g., Num. 23.22; 24.8; 2 Sam. 22.3; 2 Chron. 18.10; Ps. 18.2; Ezek. 29.21). In other words, these physical features of the Lamb cause the figures of God and Jesus to blur, as did certain details of the earlier description of Jesus in his humanoid form in Rev. 1.12-16 (compare especially the detail of Jesus' wool-like hair in 1.14 with that of God in Dan. 7.9, more on which below), and signal Revelation's 'high christology', which elevates Jesus' presumed divinity above his humanity.

Seven, however, is not the only significant number in Revelation. The book's next most important numbers are four and twelve. There are four 'living creatures' around God's heavenly throne (4.6-9; 5.6, 8, 11, 14; etc.), and when the Lamb breaks the first four seals binding the seven-sealed scroll with which he has been entrusted, four riders on four horses ride forth (6.1-8). These fearsome figures, symbolizing war, famine and other death-dealing catastrophes, are known traditionally as 'the four horsemen of the

Apocalypse', as we saw earlier. Revelation also has four angels who stand 'at the four corners of the earth [a phrase that recurs in 20.8] holding back the four winds' (7.1) – in common with many other ancient people, John conceived of the earth not as a sphere but as a square – and a further four angels 'are bound at the great river Euphrates' (9.14-15).

More prominent, however, than the number four in Revelation is its multiple, the number twelve. The New Jerusalem, the heavenly city, descended to earth, in which faithful followers of the Lamb are destined to live forever, has twelve gates guarded by twelve angels, and the names of the twelve tribes of Israel are inscribed on the gates (21.12). The wall surrounding the city has twelve foundations on which are inscribed the names of Jesus' twelve apostles (21.14). The city is 12,000 stadia (a Roman unit of measurement) in length, breadth and height (21.16), while the tree of life (transplanted from Gen. 2.9) in the middle of the city produces twelve kinds of fruit (Rev. 22.2).

Multiples of twelve also feature prominently in Revelation. In God's heavenly throne room, twenty-four elders are seated on twenty-four (secondary) thrones (4.4, 10; 5.8; 11.16; 19.4). As has often been suggested, the twenty-four elders probably stand for the twelve patriarchs of Israel (see 7.5-8) together with 'the twelve apostles of the Lamb' (see 21.14), and as such represent the entire people of God. The number of Christ followers 'sealed' or marked with God's stamp of ownership is 144,000 (7.4-8; 14.1, 3), which is to say, 12 x 12 x 1,000. And the wall surrounding the New Jerusalem is 144 cubits high (21.17), the cubit being another ancient unit of measurement.

Two other numbers in Revelation also deserve special mention. Revelation 12.6 contains a cryptic time reference: 'one thousand two hundred sixty days' (see also 11.3). This temporal period is the equivalent of the 'forty-two months' referred to in 11.2. Both derive from the 'time, two times, and half a time' – that is, three and a half years – featured in Dan. 7.25 and 12.7. In Daniel, the three and a half years appears to have literal force, according to critical scholars of the book, and begins in 167 BCE with the desecration of the Jerusalem temple by the Syrian tyrant Antiochus IV Epiphanes. In Revelation, this temporal reference is cut loose from any historical specificity, instead becoming a cipher for the indeterminate period of eschatological tribulation that must take place (see Rev. 3.10; 7.13-14; cf. Dan. 12.1) before history reaches its climax.

Revelation's most insistent numbers – four, seven, twelve and, to a lesser extent, three (for the latter, see 8.13; 9.18; 16.13, 19; 21.13, along with 11.9, 11) – may be said to symbolize for its author the divinely willed order of the cosmos. John's near contemporary, the Jewish philosopher and biblical exegete Philo of Alexandria (he died in the mid-first century CE), was also obsessed with numbers, and also assigned them divine significance. Of the number seven, for example, Philo wrote: 'Composed as it is of three and four, seven represents all that is naturally steadfast and upright in the universe' (*On the Creation* 32, Loeb trans. modified). John and Philo each stand in a Hellenistic arithmological tradition that traced itself back to the shadowy figure of the Greek philosopher-mathematician Pythagoras (see further Yarbro Collins 1996: 55–138) and ascribed sacred significance to numbers, using them to interpret human biology, the night sky and, potentially, anything whatsoever in the universe. John's relationship to the arithmological tradition is more oblique than Philo's, but he has imbibed its influence nonetheless. John uses numbers as yet another means of giving expression to his apocalyptic conviction that nothing in the fabric of the cosmos or the events of human history is arbitrary. Everything is foreseen and enclosed in the divine plan.

Who wrote Revelation?

The author of Revelation identifies himself as John (1.1, 4, 9; 22.8), a common name among ancient Jews. More precisely, John is the English form of *Iōannēs*, the name by which the author of Revelation identifies himself, and *Iōannēs* in turn was the Greek form of the ancient Hebrew name *Yôḥanan*. Through the centuries, most Christians have believed that the author of Revelation was the apostle John – that is to say, John son of Zebedee, summoned from his fishing boat by Jesus to 'fish for people' instead (Mt. 4.21-2; Mk 1.19-20; Lk. 5.9-11), and subsequently elevated by Jesus to become one of his twelve apostles (Mt. 10.2; Mk 3.14-17; Lk. 6.13-14; see also Acts 1.13; 3.1–4.22; 8.14-25; Gal. 2.6-9) – a belief that may be traced at least as far back as the mid-second century. Writing around 155 CE, Justin Martyr claims: 'There was a certain man ... whose name was John, one of Christ's apostles, who prophesied through a revelation [*en apokalypsei*] made to him that those who believed in our Christ would dwell a thousand years in Jerusalem' (*Dialogue with Trypho* 81.4, ANF trans., alluding to Rev. 20.4). Irenaeus, writing a little later, assumes without argument that the author of Revelation was John 'the Lord's disciple', the same Lord 'upon whose bosom he had leaned at supper' (*Against Heresies* 4.20.11, ANF trans., alluding to

Jn 13.23). Within the Fourth Gospel, the disciple who reclines on Jesus' chest is unnamed, but Irenaeus identifies him both as the apostle John and as the author of the gospel (*Against Heresies* 3.1.1; see also 3.16.5, 8). Irenaeus's contemporary, Clement of Alexandria, is equally convinced that the author of Revelation is 'the Apostle John' (*Who Is the Rich Man That Shall Be Saved?* 42), an identification he also feels no need to argue but only to mention, as though it is by then generally known and accepted.

Is this ancient assumption borne out by the internal evidence of Revelation? While its author does announce his name as John, three times as the book begins ('The revelation of Jesus Christ, which God ... made ... known by sending his angel to his servant John' – 1.1; 'John to the seven churches that are in Asia' – 1.4; 'I, John, your brother ..., was on the island called Patmos' – 1.9) and once again as it ends ('I, John, am the one who heard and saw these things' – 22.8), he does not identify himself as the apostle John nor does he claim apostolic authority, unlike the authors of so many of the other New Testament letters, both authentic and pseudonymous (see Rom. 1.1, 5; 11.13; 1 Cor. 1.1; 4.9; 9.1-2; 15.9; 2 Cor. 1.1; 12.12; Gal. 1.1, 17; Eph. 1.1; Col. 1.1; 1 Thess. 2.7; 1 Tim. 1.1; 2 Tim. 1.1, 11; 2.7; Tit. 1.1; 1 Pet. 1.1; 2 Pet. 1.1, 16-18). Had the author of Revelation been the apostle John, he might have claimed to have seen the earthly Jesus, as does the author of 2 Peter (1.16-18), but he claims only to have seen the risen Jesus (Rev. 1.12-16), as does the apostle Paul (1 Cor. 15.8; see also 9.1; Gal. 1.15-16). The sole mention of the twelve apostles in Revelation occurs in a context that seems to suggest that its author, like the (pseudonymous) authors of Ephesians, 2 Peter and Jude, sees them as founder figures from the past: 'And the wall of the [heavenly] city has twelve foundations, and on them are the twelve names of the twelve apostles of the Lamb' (Rev. 21.14; see also 18.20; Eph. 2.19-20; 2 Pet. 3.1-2; Jude 17-18).

Irenaeus, as we saw, writing around 180 CE, identified John of Revelation both as the apostle John and as the author of the Fourth Gospel. Doubts that the author of the Gospel of John and the Apocalypse of John were the same person, however, long preceded the advent of modern biblical criticism. Already in the mid-third century, Dionysius of Alexandria argued that Revelation, on the one hand, and the Gospel and Letters of John, on the other, cannot plausibly be ascribed to the same author. Such authorities as Irenaeus, Clement of Alexandria, Tertullian and Origen had attributed the First Letter of John to the apostle John along with the Fourth Gospel, while Irenaeus and Clement had also attributed the Second Letter of John to him.

Dionysius wrote: 'I judge from the ... entire execution of [Revelation], that it is not [the apostle John's]' (quoted in Eusebius, *Church History*

7.25.8, NPNF trans. here and below). Dionysius's comments on Revelation's Greek, in particular, are intriguing. How would a rhetorically educated, stylistically sophisticated writer of ancient Greek have reacted to Revelation's prose, in which the words are Greek but the grammar and syntax, more often than not, are Hebrew, Aramaic or otherwise nonstandard – so much so as to impel one modern interpreter of Revelation to argue that John strategically chose, for anti-imperial reasons, to write in the 'pidginized "ghetto Greek"' of his diasporic Jewish community (Callahan 1995: 454)? Dionysius's reflections on Revelation's Greek, preserved in Eusebius's *Church History*, provide a unique window on the book's reception by at least one elite ancient reader (as Dionysius seems to have been; see Feltoe 2015: 14):

> The diction of the Gospel and Epistle [1 John] differs from that of the Apocalypse. For they were written not only without error as regards the Greek language, but also with elegance in their expression .... They are far indeed from betraying any barbarism or solecism [grammatical irregularity] .... I do not deny that [the author of the Apocalypse] saw a revelation and received knowledge and prophecy. I perceive, however, that his dialect and language are not accurate Greek, but that he uses barbarous idioms, and, in some places, solecisms .... I would not have anyone think that I have said these things in a spirit of ridicule, for I have said what I have only with the purpose of showing clearly the difference between the writings.
>
> (*Church History* 7.25.24-7)

Yet Dionysius is overplaying his hand when he declares that Revelation is so 'different from these writings and foreign to them' as not to have 'a syllable in common with them' (*Church History* 7.25.22), for Revelation and the Fourth Gospel do share some theological vocabulary. Both books hail Jesus as 'the Word' (*ho logos* – Rev. 19.13; Jn 1.1, 14; see also 1 Jn 1.1) and apply to him light imagery (Rev. 21.23-4; Jn 1.4-9; 3.19-21; 8.12; 9.5; 11.9-10; 12.35-6, 46; see also 1 Jn 1.5-7; 2.8-11), living water imagery (Rev. 7.17; 22.1; Jn 4.10-14; 7.37-9) and shepherd imagery (Rev. 7.16-17; Jn 10.1-18). Both Revelation's Jesus and the Johannine Jesus utter divine pronouncements that begin with the words 'I am' (*egō eimi* – Rev. 1.17-18; 2.23b; 22.13, 16b; Jn 6.35; 8.12; 10.7, 11; 11.25; 14.6; 15.1). Most notably, the title 'Lamb', which is prominently applied to Jesus in the Fourth Gospel (1.29, 36) but not in the Synoptic Gospels, is the preeminent title for Jesus in Revelation (applied twenty-eight times to him, as we noted earlier) – although that last connection is complicated by the fact that each text employs a different Greek word for 'lamb': John uses *amnos* but Revelation uses *arnion*.

Much knottier complications are also in play. The shared theological vocabulary of Revelation and the Fourth Gospel is notoriously difficult to explain, because in relation to the theme of eschatology, Revelation's pervasive preoccupation, the two books are worlds apart theologically. In particular, Jesus' return in glory is of towering importance in Revelation (see 19.11-16 together with 1.7; 3.11; 16.15; 22.7, 12, 20), but the Fourth Gospel shows almost no interest in Jesus' return, relative not just to Revelation but also to the Synoptic Gospels, or in any future-oriented eschatology.

Even on theological grounds, then, and overwhelming on stylistic grounds, Revelation and the Fourth Gospel do not appear to stem from the same author. What else can we know about the writer of Revelation? While the author, or authors, of the Fourth Gospel is, or are, anonymous, the author of Revelation is not: 'I, John ... '. This name does not appear to be pseudonymous. Unlike the author of, say, the Letter to the Ephesians, the Pastoral Epistles or the Second Letter of Peter – or, for that matter, the *Apocalypse of Peter* or the *Apocalypse of Paul* – the author of Revelation is not claiming the authority of a dead apostolic hero from an idealized Christian past in order to make his pronouncements. Since the author does not identify himself as the apostle John, Revelation cannot be labelled a pseudonymous work. That makes Revelation one of only two known apocalypses, whether Jewish or Christian, from antiquity that can plausibly be regarded as non-pseudonymous (the *Shepherd of Hermas* being the other candidate, an early Christian work, loosely apocalyptic in genre, that appears to have achieved its final form in the mid-second century). The author of Revelation speaks confidently in his own name and solely with the authority his claimed visions confer on him.

John represents himself as receiving his initial or commissioning (1.11, 19) vision on Patmos ('I ... was on the island called Patmos' – 1.9), one of the hundreds of inhabitable islands that dot the Aegean Sea between the eastern and northeastern coasts of Greece and the western coast of what is now Turkey. With an area of only 13 square miles, Patmos is a small island about 40 miles from the Turkish mainland and about 60 miles southwest of the ruins of the ancient city of Ephesus, whose Christian assembly is the first to be addressed by Revelation's Son of Man (2.1-7). John tells us that he was on Patmos 'because of the word of God and the testimony of Jesus' (1.9). The tradition that John had been exiled or banished to Patmos is common in the writings of ancient church authorities. Clement of Alexandria, to cite what may be the earliest extant example, writing near the end of the second or early third century, remarks in passing: 'On the tyrant's death, he [John] returned to Ephesus from the island of Patmos' (*Who Is the Rich Man That Shall Be Saved?* 42, ANF trans.). Clement's unnamed tyrant is commonly taken to be the Roman Emperor Domitian, who died in 96 CE. In a work written by Tertullian around the same time or a little later, we encounter a lurid embellishment of John's legend: he is 'plunged, unhurt, into boiling oil' in Rome – after which he is exiled to Patmos (*Prescriptions against Heretics* 36, ANF trans.). Writing around 260 CE, Victorinus of Pettau influentially fleshes out the alleged exile: '[John] was on the island of Patmos, condemned to the labor of the mines by the emperor Domitian' (*Commentary on the Apocalypse* 10.11, ANF trans.).

There is no evidence that Patmos was a Roman penal colony (see Boxall 2013: 38), which is what Victorinus seems to imagine. What, then, was John doing on Patmos? Why was he on the island if he hadn't been condemned to hard labour there? To evangelize the locals? In addition to the inherent unlikelihood that John would turn his back on the vast missionary territories of the mainland in order to evangelize a small island far from the coast, John tells us that he was on Patmos 'because of the word of God [*dia ton logon tou theou*] and the testimony of Jesus' (1.9), and commentators have long noted both that the Greek preposition *dia* followed by the accusative, as here, is used elsewhere in Revelation only to denote the result of an action, not its purpose (John is on Patmos *because of* his preaching or prophesying, in other words, not *in order to* preach or prophesy); and that in two other instances in Revelation (6.9; 20.4), persecution is the direct result of proclaiming the word of God and testifying to Jesus. John may have been on the island, then, either because he was hiding from the authorities on the mainland or because he had been exiled there by those authorities – that is, the governing authorities of the Roman province of Asia, under whose jurisdiction Patmos fell.

Several scholars have made compelling cases that the ancient tradition claiming John had been exiled to Patmos is historically plausible (see esp. Aune 1997: 78–80; Oster 2013: 65–8; Koester 2014: 242–3). The specific punishment inflicted on John by the Roman authorities in Asia (so these arguments go)

was probably 'relegation to an island' (*relegatio ad insulam*). Under this sentence deportation was usually temporary and did not entail the loss of Roman citizenship or property, though in some cases it was permanent and involved a loss of property (Pliny the Younger, *Ep.* 10.56.3-4). The person could not leave the island but could associate with people there and could receive support from family and friends (Philostratus, *Vit. Apoll.* 7.16.2; Philo, *Flacc.* 166). A more severe punishment was 'deportation to an island' (*deportatio*

ad insulam), which was permanent and entailed the loss of property ....
The sentence of relegation could be given by the provincial proconsul if an
island was in his jurisdiction (Justinian, *Dig.* 48.22.7.1) .... Deportation had
to be imposed by the emperor.... So it is likely that John was relegated by the
provincial authorities rather than deported.

(Koester 2014: 242)

If John had indeed been 'relegated' to Patmos, the possible implications for
his social status are interesting. The Roman judicial system seems to have
reserved relegation to an island for persons of high social standing (Justinian,
Digest 48.19.38.2-9; see also 48.19.27.1). If John was such a person, he may
have renounced his wealth and privileges (whether or not he was formally
stripped of them by the Roman state), as is suggested by his critical stance
on wealth in Rev. 3.17-18 and especially 18.11-20.

When was Revelation written?

The Roman Empire is the largest target in John of Patmos's polemical sights.
But in which moment of Roman history is John writing? Against which
configuration of Roman imperial power does he counterpose his Messianic
Empire (see 11.15)? In attempting to ascribe a date of composition to
Revelation, critical scholars rely principally on Revelation 13 and 17. But
these chapters are also the primary reason why scholars read Revelation as
anti-Roman invective in the first place.

Revelation 13 is a vision of two beasts, as we have already seen, a sea beast
(13.1-2) and a land beast (13.11). The sea beast – part leopard, part bear and
part lion, with multiple heads and horns – is a composite creation, a fusion
of the four separate beasts beheld by the prophet Daniel in a dream (Dan.
7.2-7). The sea beast appears again in Rev. 17.3, now with a mysterious figure
seated on it: 'I saw a woman sitting on a scarlet beast that ... had seven heads
and ten horns' (cf. 13.1). In Rev. 17.9 the beast is implicitly identified as
Rome. We are told that its seven heads represent seven *orē* ('the seven heads
are seven *orē* on which the woman is seated'), a Greek word that may equally
be translated 'hills' or 'mountains'. Rome was popularly known as 'the city of
seven hills', as ancient literature amply attests, the Latin poet Propertius, for
instance, declaiming: 'High on its seven hills, the city that rules the whole
world' (*Elegies* 3.11.57). But the heads also represent seven *basileis* (Rev.
17.9), Greek for 'emperors' or 'kings'. These details in combination invite an
interpretation of the sea beast as a symbol for Rome and its emperors.

The sea beast is not the only symbol for Rome in Revelation. The woman mounted on the beast is introduced in detail in Rev. 17.1-6, having received passing mention earlier in 14.8 and 16.19. Her description as 'drunk with the blood of the saints and the blood of the witnesses to Jesus' (17.6), coupled with her identification as 'the great city that rules over the kings of the earth' (17.18), suggests that she too represents imperial Rome. This is further intimated by her name, which is said to be Babylon: 'On her forehead was written a name, a mystery: "Babylon the great, mother of whores and of earth's abominations"' (17.5; cf. 14.8; 16.19; 18.2, 10, 21). The historical Babylon (or, more precisely, the Neo-Babylonian Empire of which the city Babylon was the capital) destroyed the first Jerusalem temple, built by King Solomon, in 586 BCE (see 2 Kgs 25.8-9; 2 Chron. 36.17-19; Jer. 52.12-13). Rome in turn destroyed the rebuilt or second temple in 70 CE, thereby becoming, in Jewish and Jewish-Christian eyes, the new Babylon. Indeed, Babylon is a code word for Rome not only in Revelation but also in other ancient apocalyptic literature (*4 Ezra* 3.1-2, 28-31; *2 Baruch* 10.1-3; 11.1; 67.7; see also *Sibylline Oracles* 5.143, 159) and in the First Letter of Peter (5.13).

Revelation's use of the name Babylon as a cipher for Rome features prominently in the scholarly debate over Revelation's final date of composition. Many scholars see Revelation's symbolic use of the name Babylon as evidence that the book is post-70 CE, and use a statement by Irenaeus to date it more precisely to the mid-90s CE. Writing around 180 CE, Irenaeus claimed that John 'beheld the apocalyptic vision ... toward the end of Domitian's reign' (*Against Heresies* 5.30.3). Domitian was emperor from 81 to 96 CE. Irenaeus does not say specifically that John *wrote* his book near the end of Domitian's reign, as opposed to at a later date. Given, however, that John represents himself repeatedly as being peremptorily ordered to commit what he is being shown or told to writing (1.11, 19; 2.1, 8, 12, 18; 3.1, 7, 14; 10.4; 14.13; 19.9; 21.5), it is probably safe to surmise that Irenaeus did not imagine any significant delay between the vision and the book.

Other elements in Revelation, however, seem to suggest an earlier date of composition than that evoked by Irenaeus, as we shall gradually see, in particular 'the number of the beast' in 13.18: 'Let anyone with understanding calculate the number of the beast, for it is the number of a person. Its number is six hundred sixty-six' (cf. 13.17; 15.2). Revelation 13.18 is an instance of the ancient practice known as *gematria* in Hebrew and *isopsephy* in Greek: the assigning of numeric values to names or other words. The popularity of the practice is attested by its use in ancient graffiti. Isopsephic graffiti have been discovered in the ruins of Pergamum and Smyrna, two of Revelation's seven cities, as well as in the ruins of the Italian city of Pompeii. Particularly arresting in this lover's graffito unearthed in Pompeii: 'I love her whose number is 545'. Closer to Rev. 13.18, as we shall see, is an elaborate anti-imperial graffito that the ancient historian Suetonius (*Nero* 39.2) tells us was written on Rome's city wall:

> Count the numerical values
> Of the letters in Nero's name,
> And in 'murdered his own mother'
> You'll find their sum is the same.

> (Graves 1957 trans.)

So how did gematria or isopsephy work? The symbols used for numbers in the contemporary West and much of the rest of the world (technically, the Hindu-Arabic numeral system) did not exist in the ancient world. Instead, the letters in many ancient alphabets doubled as numbers. In both Hebrew and Greek, for instance, the first ten letters of each alphabet represented the numbers one through ten, and the eleventh and subsequent letters represented multiples of ten. As it happens, the name Nero Caesar (Caesar being one of the names Nero adopted on ascending to the throne – a name that, by then, was well on its way to becoming a formal imperial title) written in Hebrew (a language with which the author of Revelation shows signs of being deeply familiar) yields the number 666. The Hebrew form of Nero Caesar is *nrôn qsr*, and when each letter is accorded its numerical value ($n = 50$; $r = 200$; $ô = 6$; $n = 50$; $q = 100$; $s = 60$; $r = 200$) and the resulting string of numbers is added up, the total is 666.

Given that the beast is identified as Rome and seven of its emperors in Rev. 17.9, as we saw, what does it mean that the beast is identified as the Emperor Nero in 13.18? Arguably, it suggests that Nero epitomized for John, embodied like no other, the evil of imperial Rome. General persecution of Christ-followers looms large in Revelation (6.9; 7.14; 12.17; 13.7-10, 15-17; 17.6; 18.24; 19.2; 20.4), sounding a prophetic alert more than reflecting a present reality, as numerous scholars have noted – although John also references specific persecutions that the Christian assemblies in his seven churches have recently experienced (2.3, 9-10, 13; 3.8; see also 1.9). Whenever Revelation may plausibly be said to have been written, however, Nero was still the Roman emperor responsible for the most severe persecution of Christians that had yet been unleashed. The ancient Roman historian Tacitus famously describes that mass persecution:

> To stop the rumor [that he himself had started the great fire of Rome], Nero created scapegoats and punished with every refinement the notoriously depraved 'Christians' .... First, Nero had the self-confessed Christians arrested. Then, on their information, large numbers of others were condemned .... Their deaths were made a source of entertainment. Dressed in wild animal skins, they were torn to pieces by dogs, or crucified, or made into torches to be set on fire after dark as illumination. (*Annals of Imperial Rome* 15.47, Grant 1971 trans.; see also Suetonius, *Nero* 16.2; 38.1)

Small wonder that Nero is a sinister presence in Revelation, if Tacitus's account of his atrocities against Christ-followers is even partially accurate.

The decryption of 666 as a coded reference to Nero also enables scholars to make sense of an enigmatic detail in the description of the sea beast. One of its seven heads 'seemed to have received a death-blow, but its mortal wound had been healed' (Rev. 13.3; see also 13.12). Nero committed suicide in 68 CE, slitting his throat, aided by his secretary, after hearing that the Roman Senate had formally declared him an enemy of the people and sentenced him to a torturous death (Suetonius, *Nero* 49.2-4; see also Cassius Dio, *Roman History* 63.29.2). Few, however, saw Nero's corpse, and the rumour spread that he had not really died but was in hiding and would return to Rome to regain his throne and take revenge on his enemies. Between 68 (or 69) and 88 CE, at least three Nero imposters appeared (Tacitus, *Histories* 2.8-9; Suetonius, *Nero* 57.1-2; Cassius Dio, *Roman History* 66.19.3). Critical interpreters of Revelation have long conjectured that Nero's forced suicide is the 'death blow' of 13.3, and the 'healing' of that 'mortal wound' (13.3, 12) is the popular anticipation of his return (the myth of Nero *redivivus*, as it is called). If so, John likely sees Nero's apparent overcoming of death as a satanic parody of Jesus' resurrection. Like the risen Jesus, the Nero-beast might declare, 'I was dead, and behold, I am alive' (Rev. 1.18; see also 2.8). The beast also seems to possess further parodic divine traits. The thrice-repeated assertion that the beast 'was and is not and is to come' (which, with variations, crops up twice in 17.8 and again in 17.11) appears to parody the thrice-repeated acclamation of God as the one 'who is and who was and who is to come' (1.4, 8; 4.8).

Nero's relative prominence in Revelation 13 has led a number of scholars to argue for a date of composition for Revelation shortly after his death, especially in light of Rev. 17.9-11:

> This calls for a mind that has wisdom: the seven heads [of the beast] are seven mountains [or hills: *orē*] on which the woman [Babylon] is seated; also they are seven kings [or emperors: *basileis*], of whom five have fallen, one is living,

and the other has not yet come; and when he comes, he must remain only a little while. As for the beast that was and is not, it is an eighth but it belongs to the seven, and it goes to destruction.

How best to decrypt this riddle? If we begin the count of the seven *basileis* with Augustus, the first true Roman emperor, the 'five [who] have fallen' would then be Augustus, Tiberius, Gaius (better known by his nickname Caligula), Claudius and Nero. The 'one [who] is living' would be Nero's successor, Galba, whose brief reign extended from June 68 to January 69 CE. Some scholars argue that John wrote during Galba's reign, although they must then make sense of 'the other [who] has not yet come; and … must remain only a little while'. The death of Nero, the last emperor of the Julio-Claudian dynasty established by Augustus, unleashed civil war. Galba's was only the first of three truncated imperial reigns – his successors Otho and Vitellius reigned only for three and eight months respectively – and perhaps the originator of Rev. 7.9-11 (whether John himself or some earlier source) had seen the writing on the wall during the tumultuous reign of Galba, realizing that a return to political stability was not in the immediate future. As for the final element of the riddle, 'the eighth [who] belongs to the seven' and 'goes to destruction', that appears to be a further reference to the myth of Nero *redivivus*. On this reading, Nero would be both the fifth of the seven emperors and the last emperor, the eighth – the eschatological one who, as 'the beast … from the bottomless pit' (11.7; 17.8), is destined to be 'thrown alive into the lake of fire that burns with sulfur' (19.20).

All in all, those who argue for a date of composition for Revelation shortly after Nero's reign (post-68 CE) have an easier time making sense of 17.9-11 than those who argue for a date near the end of Domitian's reign (pre-96 CE). Domitian was the eleventh Roman emperor, counting from Augustus. Some fancy footwork is needed in interpreting 17.9-11 to get all the way down to Domitian, such as not counting the three short-reigning emperors Galba, Otho and Vitellius. Vespasian, then (Vitellius's successor and the founder of a new dynasty, the Flavian), would be the sixth emperor, the 'one [who] is living', reigning when the author purports to be writing; his son Titus, who reigned only from 79 to 81 CE, would be the one who 'must remain only a little while'; and Titus's brother Domitian would be 'the eighth [who] belongs to the seven', which is to say the new Nero. But since the author knows about Titus and Domitian, on this reading, he is only pretending to write during the reign of Vespasian; he is really writing during the reign of Domitian.

Advocates for the later date sometimes attempt to avoid such headache-inducing complications by doing an end run around Rev. 17.9-11 altogether, arguing that seven is once again the symbolic number of totality here, representing the entire line of Roman emperors up until the time in which John is writing (whenever that might be). To ask which emperors exactly are included in the seven, on this interpretation, is to miss the symbolic point of the number. The specificity, however, of the narrative details appended to the statement 'the seven heads [of the beast] ... are seven emperors' ('of whom five have fallen, one is living, and the other ... when he comes ... must remain only a little while') militates against the elegance of the symbolic-number solution and continues to seduce the scholarly imagination to attach names to the numbers.

Proponents of the early date also point to Rev. 11.1-2 ('I was told, "Come and measure the temple of God and the altar and those who worship there"') and argue that it indicates the Jerusalem temple is still standing as John writes, and so we have not yet arrived at 70 CE when the temple was destroyed by Titus and his legions. Proponents of the late date often respond that the temple in question is not the earthly temple. Instead, it is either the heavenly temple, frequently mentioned elsewhere in Revelation (7.15; 11.19; 14.15, 17; 15.5-6, 8; 16.1, 17), or a symbol for the Christian community (see 3.12) – although again, as with 17.9-11, there is a surfeit of additional detail that is difficult to fold into the simpler explanations: 'Come and measure the temple of God and the altar and those who worship there, but do not measure the court outside the temple; leave that out, for it is given over to the Gentiles [*tois ethnesin*; to the Romans?], and they will trample over the holy city for forty-two months.'

All told, those championing the early date might be thought to have the better argument of it were it not for Revelation's extensive use of the code name Babylon for Rome. Use of this code name, as explained above, seems to point to a date after the Roman destruction of the Jerusalem temple, which is to say, post-70 CE. A compromise position that circumvents the early date/late date dichotomy, but is less common than one might expect, sees Revelation in its final form as stemming from the late first (or early second) century (depending on how much credence one accords to Irenaeus's claim that John had his vision near the end of Domitian's reign), but as incorporating certain material that originated much earlier and that John is merely channelling, such as that concerning Nero and the temple.

Why was Revelation written?

As is evident from much of what we have been saying, Revelation is anti-imperial resistance literature at base. That is the main reason for Revelation – its why, its raison d'être. One would, indeed, be hard pressed to name in all of ancient literature a more vitriolic critique of Rome than that found in Revelation. But what is it about Rome that John finds so objectionable?

Revelation 18 suggests one answer to this question. The anticipatory celebration of imperial Rome's fall in this chapter ('Fallen, fallen is Babylon the great!' – 18.2; cf. Isa. 21.9) is a celebration of the collapse of an *economic* empire (see Rev. 18.3c, 7a, 9, 11-19, 23c). The celebration is couched in the form of mock laments or 'taunt songs', closely modelled on those of the Hebrew prophets (e.g., Isa. 14.4-21; Jer. 50.8-16). In and through these mock laments, the merchant class emerges as the main beneficiary of Rome's economic empire: 'The merchants … who gained wealth from her [Babylon/Rome] will stand far off …, weeping and mourning aloud, "Alas, alas, the great city …. For in one hour all this wealth has been laid waste!"' (Rev. 18.15-17a; see also 18.11-14, 17b-19). The merchants' wealth derives from their greedy willingness to strip the earth and exploit its peoples in order to feed affluent Romans' insatiable appetite for luxury goods.

Revelation 18.11-13 contains an itemized list of these luxury goods, the so-called cargo list, with slaves bringing up the rear – arguably, the closest any New Testament text comes to a critique of the slave system on which the Roman economy was founded, slavery here being implicitly condemned as the objectification and commodification of human beings (contrast Eph. 6.5-6; Col. 3.22; 1 Tim. 6.1; Tit. 2.9-10):

> And the merchants of the earth weep and mourn for her, since no one buys their cargo anymore, cargo of gold, silver, jewels, and pearls, fine linen, purple, silk and scarlet, all kinds of scented wood, all articles of ivory, all articles of costly wood, bronze, iron, and marble, cinnamon, spice, incense, myrrh, frankincense, wine, olive oil, choice flour and wheat, cattle and sheep, horses and chariots, slaves – and human lives.
>
> (Rev. 18.11-13)

The final words of the cargo list may be rendered more literally as: ' … and horses and chariots and bodies [*sōmatōn*, a synonym for "slaves" elsewhere in Greco Roman literature and inscriptions], that is to say, human lives/souls [*kai psychas anthrōpōn*]' – or, in contemporary idiom, 'human beings'.

All told, Revelation 18 may be read as a ringing critique of the economic exploitation on which Rome's empire was based (see further Bauckham 1993; Míguez 1995; Park 2008), exploitation that ravaged the nonhuman world and preyed on the most vulnerable populations of the human world.

John has other problems with Rome in addition to his outrage about its economic injustices. His reference to 'blasphemous names' on the heads of the beast ('I saw a beast rising out of the sea … and on its heads were blasphemous names' – 13.1; see also 17.3) is telling. As we saw, these heads represent Roman emperors (see 17.9). The 'blasphemous names', then, beg to be interpreted as the honorific titles applied to Roman emperors, living and dead – titles such as 'God', 'Son of God', 'Savior of the World' and, eventually, 'Lord'. Note in addition the repeated references in Revelation to the worship of the beast (13.4, 8, 12, 15; 14.9, 11; 16.2; 19.20; 20.4; see also 9.20). At issue here is the practice and institution of emperor worship, the Roman imperial cult, as it is called.

The cult was instituted in 42 BCE when Julius Caesar – dictator of the Roman Republic (his official title) and architect of the Roman Empire – was declared divine by the Roman Senate following his assassination. Each of Caesar's successors, beginning with his adopted son Octavian, honorifically renamed Augustus, had his own distinctive relationship to divinity. Some emperors, such as Tiberius, were not eager for divine honours (although Tiberius did not object to them in principle, it seems). Other emperors, such as Caligula and Nero, embraced them greedily. In the city of Rome itself, divine honours were normally extended only to deceased emperors. In certain of the Roman provinces, most of all the eastern provinces, the worship of living emperors was common.

Revelation is addressed to seven churches in the Roman province of Asia (1.4a, 10-11), as we have seen. From an early stage, the cities of Asia enthusiastically embraced the Roman imperial cult. Already in 29 BCE, the Assembly of Asia, made up of delegates from the principal Asian cites, requested and was granted the honour of building a special temple jointly dedicated to the Emperor Augustus and the goddess Roma, the divine personification of the city of Rome. The temple was located in Pergamum, one of Revelation's seven cities (2.12-17). It has often been suggested that 'Satan's throne' in Rev. 2.13 ('I know where you are living, where Satan's throne is', the risen Jesus declares to the Pergamum church) is a cryptic reference to the temple of Augustus and Roma. Also in 29 BCE, a temple to Roma and Julius Caesar was dedicated in Ephesus, another of Revelation's seven cities (2.1-7). Meanwhile, the temple to Roma in Smyrna, yet another of the seven cities (2.8-11), had stood since 195 BCE, the first such temple in the Roman world. In 26 CE, Smyrna added a temple dedicated to the Emperor Tiberius and the Roman Senate. In due course, each of Revelation's seven cities, along with others in the province of Asia, erected temples or altars to Roman potentates, living or dead, or to Roman world-conquering military might in general, as personified by the warrior goddess Roma who was ordinarily represented in armour and often as triumphantly enthroned upon the weapons of the armies she has vanquished. Small wonder that Asia was one of the 'ungarrisoned' provinces of the empire, meaning that no full legions of Roman troops were stationed within its borders, or needed to be. The leading Asian cities manoeuvred adroitly to turn their subservience to Rome to their advantage, competing with each other to offer extravagant honours to the emperor and receive imperial benefactions in return.

For this well-oiled religiopolitical machine, a major driver of which was the temples and festivals of the imperial cult, John of Revelation has nothing but contempt. 'Worshiping the beast' (13.4, 8, 12, 15; 14.9, 11; 16.2; 19.20; 20.4; cf. 9.20) is John's term of derision for the imperial cult. For John, indeed, emperor worship is tantamount to devil worship: 'They worshiped the dragon [i.e., Satan; see 12.9; 20.2], for he had given his authority to the beast, and they worshiped the beast' (13.4; see also 13.8). 'The' beast is really the sea beast ('I saw a beast rising out of the sea' – 13.1), which is distinct from the land beast ('I saw another beast that rose out of the earth' – 13.11), the second beast of Revelation 13, as we have seen. The function of the land beast is to cause 'the earth and its inhabitants [to] worship the first beast' (13.12-15), that is, the sea beast, which, as we have also seen, is Rome and its emperors (or, more precisely perhaps, the Roman emperors as the absolute embodiment of Rome's imperial power). It has often been suggested, therefore, that the land beast represents the priesthood responsible for the implementation and administration of the Roman imperial cult, particularly in the province of Asia.

What did the imperial cult mean for Christ-followers? In certain circumstances, life or death. An official letter from around 112 CE details the potential consequences of refusing to worship the emperor. In the letter, Pliny, governor of Bithynia, which bordered the province of Asia, explains to the Emperor Trajan that persons denounced to him as Christians are, among other tests of loyalty to the Roman state, ordered to make offerings of wine and incense to a statue of the emperor – to 'worship your image', as Pliny puts it. Failure to do so results in death (Pliny, *Letters* 10.96; cf. Rev. 13.15; 20.4).

Yet the crisis situation represented in Pliny's letter would have been the exception rather than the rule for the Christian assemblies addressed in Revelation. (One such exception is named in the letter to Pergamum: 'You did not deny your faith in me even in the days of Antipas my witness, my faithful one, who was killed among you, where Satan lives' – 2.13.) Christ-followers could choose to assimilate to certain socioreligious norms and thereby lessen their risk of being denounced as unpatriotic or seditious. Such manoeuvrability would have been afforded by the fact that the imperial cult was not forcibly imposed from above by the Roman state on the populace of Asia. Generally speaking, the cult was an object of eager embrace rather than coerced compliance, and not only by civic leaders who stood to gain the most from it in terms of Roman favour and benefaction. Imperial festivals were a prominent feature of the religious life of Asia and were popular with the common people.

Assertions of the emperor's divine status also permeated more mundane aspects of daily life. In particular, commerce and religion were inextricably intertwined, beginning with the fact that many Roman coins carried inscriptions declaring the divinity of one or other emperor. For instance, notwithstanding Tiberius's well-documented reluctance to accept divine honours, every gold, silver or bronze coin minted during his reign proclaims him *divi filius* or *theou huios*, 'son of the god', the god in question being the deified Augustus (who himself had qualified for the same title as adoptive son of the deified Julius Caesar); and *divi filius* coins were also struck to honour certain subsequent emperors, notably Nero and Domitian. For reasons such as these, Revelation's critique of the Roman economic system (see esp. 18.11-19) cannot be separated from its critique of the Roman imperial cult (see esp. 13.16-17).

Why, in more general terms, was Revelation written? More than anything else, it was written as a warning – but not as a warning of physical peril. For the author of Revelation, the central crisis facing Asian Christ-followers is not that they might be arrested and even executed for their faith. The central crisis facing Asian Christ-followers is rather the temptation to accommodate themselves to Roman culture in its immensely seductive socioreligious and religioeconomic forms, a culture John sees as abhorrently idolatrous and deeply unjust. Such accommodation is, for John, precisely the sin of 'Jezebel' and her followers (2.18-25; see also 2.14-15), to which we shall return in Chapter 4. John's impassioned message to the Asian Christian assembles is that Rome, notwithstanding – or because of – its captivating culture, is destined for divine destruction, and so they must 'come out of her' (18.4) lest they share her fiery fate. For the fate of Rome, the imperial city, and the fate of Rome's loyal subjects, an important vehicle of whose patriotism was the imperial cult, are ultimately identical in Revelation: 'And the kings of the earth … [will] see the smoke of her [Babylon/Rome's] burning; they will stand far off in fear of her torment' (18.9-10; cf. 17.16; 18.8, 17b-18; 19.20; 20.10); 'Those who worship the beast and its image … will be tormented with fire and sulfur …. And the smoke of their torment goes up forever and ever' (14.9-11; cf. 20.15; 21.8).

And yet, even amid the sickening stench of burning flesh, smoke stinging our eyes, we should not lose sight of the fact that, as noted above, the book of Revelation is the most uncompromising critique of imperial Rome – or, arguably, of (human) empire in general – to emerge from the ancient world. For this reason, as also noted earlier, Revelation has been a crucial biblical resource for liberation theology, that unapologetically political mode of theologizing centrally concerned with economic justice. Revelation has regularly been read by liberationists as the quintessential biblical critique of empire, whether ancient or modern. Relatedly, they have also found Revelation to be singularly well equipped to speak to situations of state-sponsored oppression, notwithstanding the fact that empirewide, state-sponsored persecution of Christians was still a relatively distant phenomenon when Revelation was written. Sporadic local persecution of Christians would have been the reality when John penned his apocalypse, as scholars have argued repeatedly in recent decades. John writes, however, as though mass persecution was an imminent reality (see esp. 6.9-11; 7.9, 13-14; 12.11, 17; 17.6; 18.24; 20.4), and his book derives much of its rhetorical power from this crisis-conjuring stance. Consequently, it has always had the capacity to comfort and orient Christians faced with systemic oppression.

4

A micro-commentary on Revelation

My micro-commentary on Revelation is also of necessity a partial commentary. I do not comment on every scene in the book, nor could I. Instead, I will focus on certain scenes that interest me the most, scenes that repeatedly provoke me to thought.

'I saw one like a genderqueer person of color'

From its first pages, Revelation bristles with bizarre details and seethes with surreal spectacles. The book's prologue (1.1-8) is followed by its opening vision, the appearance to John of 'one like a son of man [*huios anthrōpou*]' (1.13), who, we are told, commissions John to write the book (1.11, 19) in which we read of the vision. The 'one like a son of man' has stepped out of another book, as it happens, the book of Daniel. In that book, the protagonist has a vision in which he sees 'one like a son of man [*bar-'ĕnāš*] coming with the clouds of heaven' (7.13). In Revelation, this numinous being materializes on the island of Patmos (1.9) and receives a head-to-toe description from John. As we noted earlier, Rev. 1.12-16 is the only physical description of Jesus contained in the New Testament (other than the minimalist sketches of his transfigured appearance in Mt. 17.2, Mk 9.2-3, and Lk. 9.29). Of course, it is the risen and glorified Christ who is described in Revelation ('I was dead, and see, I am alive forever and ever' – Rev. 1.18), not Jesus of Nazareth, the Galilean peasant.

Revelation is not the only early Christian narrative whose Jesus is already dead and risen on its first page. Within the New Testament, this is also true of the Acts of the Apostles (1.1-11), in addition to several extracanonical Christian texts conventionally labelled 'Gnostic', such as *The Acts of Peter and the Twelve Apostles* and *The Secret Book of John*. Another sibling text, *The Sophia of Jesus Christ*, presents an interesting contrast with Revelation's opening vision. It begins with the risen Jesus appearing to his closest disciples, but 'not in his previous form'. His likeness rather 'resembles a great angel of light. But his resemblance I must not describe', the anonymous author adds, 'no mortal flesh could endure it' (Parrott 1990 trans.). John of Revelation, too, is overwhelmed by what he sees – 'When I saw him, I fell at his feet as though dead' (1.17) – but presents us with a detailed description of the unearthly figure nonetheless, a figure who, as it turns out, is also thoroughly angelic (see Carrell 1997: 129–74).

The falling-in-a-faint motif is a convention of apocalyptic literature, and the entity who elicits that response from John is himself assembled from prior apocalyptic texts, most notably Dan. 10.5-6. Daniel's vision in this instance is of an angelic being, most likely the archangel Gabriel (see 8.15-17; 9.20-1). On Daniel's description of this glorious figure John models his own description of the glorified Jesus. Like Daniel's angel, John's Jesus wears a golden belt, has flaming eyes and feet like burnished bronze (Dan. 10.5-6; Rev. 1.13-15). It is not, however, that the risen Jesus is himself an angel, pure and simple, in Revelation. John's initial description of Jesus merges two Danielic figures, as we have seen, the 'one like a son of man' (Dan. 7.13-14) and an angelic interpreter (10.5-6); but John also folds a third Danielic figure into the description, the 'Ancient One' (Dan. 7.9-10) who is the god of Israel. Like Daniel's Ancient One who has 'hair like pure wool' (7.9), John's Jesus has hair 'white as white wool' (Rev. 1.14). The innocuous-seeming detail of the white hair transforms John's Jesus from an angel into a god. What is the significance of this transmutation? John will later make a special point – twice, in fact – of insisting that angels must not be worshipped (19.9-10; 22.8-9; cf. Col. 2.18), while presenting Jesus as eminently eligible for worship (Rev. 5.8-14; 22.3). Nevertheless, God, Jesus and angels merge in Revelation (and not just in the scene we have been considering: 10.1-3 is another prime example of such fusion); they flow in and out of each other, swap roles and trade traits.

In John's visionary introduction to Jesus, then, and throughout much of the narrative that follows, the human (for the figure John beholds, for all its divine numinosity, does have a human form) is elevated, is amalgamated with the angelic and the divine. And yet the nonhuman animal is not neglected in this transmutational ascent, to gaze forlornly heavenwards at an apotheosis of the human from which it is excluded. The animal, too, will soon be pulled fully into the heavenly orbit, as we shall see. And what of Jesus of Nazareth? What of the Galilean peasant, the product of a backwater region of a minor Roman province and of a colonized and despised ethnic group? Has he utterly vanished, been entirely consumed in the heavenly being whom John conjures up in the opening vision of his narrative? Yes and no. Jesus of Nazareth is indeed dead from the first page of Revelation. And yet John's description of the risen Jesus is one in which many marginalized people, themselves members of colonized or otherwise oppressed ethnic groups, have found themselves reflected.

Specifically, the physical characteristics of the Jesus whom John describes as having hair like wool and feet like burnished bronze are ones to which many people of African descent have gravitated, including at least one African American New Testament scholar. In his commentary on Revelation, Brian K. Blount remarks that the wool-like texture of the hair ascribed to the one like a son of man is arresting, and not only because it evokes Daniel's description of the divine Ancient One:

> In the cosmopolitan Roman Empire (and no doubt in Daniel's context as well), where people with hair like wool (e.g., Africans), were well known, it is interesting that Christ (and the Ancient of Days before him) is depicted this way, rather than with the straight hair commonly associated with those of European descent. The Gospels do not give any physical descriptions of Jesus; Revelation gives just this one. It is provocative, to say the least. (Blount 2009: 44; see also Blount 2007: 526–7)

Others have latched onto these details more determinedly, unhampered by scholarly restraint. Among the many individuals and communities in Africa and the African diaspora for whom Rev. 1.14-15 has held special significance, the Rastafari, a globally dispersed Afrocentric religious community whose origins lie in Jamaica, are particularly notable for their strategic deployment of these verses to counter the long Eurocentric tradition of erasing the presence of dark-skinned people from biblical history and whitening the figure of Jesus in particular. As Sarah Daynes (2010: 106–7) explains, 'this verse … constitutes the major argument advanced by the rastas to prove that Jesus was not a white man: if he is described in the Bible as having hair "like white wool" and feet "like burnished bronze", it is because indeed his hair was frizzy and his skin black'.

Within US culture, the detail of the woolly hair is enshrined in a memorable conversation in Alice Walker's Pulitzer Prize winning novel *The Color Purple* (1982). Celie and Shug, two African American women in rural Georgia in an unspecified decade of the early twentieth century, are debating what God and Jesus look like. Shug takes Celie to task for her inherited image of God as an 'old white man', arguing that this internalized image is purely a product of 'the white folks' white bible'. Celie concedes that she has heard from her sister Nettie that somewhere in the Bible it says that Jesus' hair 'was like lamb's wool', which prompts Shug to joke that were this Jesus ever to show up in any of the churches they frequent, he would need to get his hair straightened if he wanted to be taken seriously (1982: 194–5). By the late 1960s, as Jeffrey Ogbar (2004: 155) notes, many black churches in the United States were commissioning artistic representations of a dark-skinned Jesus, as more and more African Americans 'referenced [Rev.] 1:14-15 to affirm their belief that the historical Jesus shared the "bronze" complexion and wooly hair of black people'.

Yet Revelation has also been employed, even within black communities, to exclude certain black bodies. As queer-of-colour New Testament scholar Eric A. Thomas (2018: 90) notes, although Revelation is an important theocultural resource for 'articulations of liberation, divine vindication, and eschatological salvation ... stem[ming] from postcolonial and post-Emancipation people of African descent ..., for the most part, Africana queer experience [has been] sealed beneath those articulations and silenced'. Within Revelation itself, such exclusion comes to trenchant expression in 22.15: 'Outside' (*exō*) the heavenly city, forever excluded from it, is a list of undesirables that begins with 'the dogs' (*hoi kynes*), a term that even certain critical scholars of the New Testament and many more nonscholarly interpreters read as an epithet for sexually deviant persons, as Thomas observes (2018: 96). He remarks: 'The threat of being excluded from heaven (the New Jerusalem) presented by the text of Revelation and its homophobic heteronormative interpreters in the *future* is moot for Africana queer people whose lives, as the result of homo- and transphobic violence and rejection, are a living hell in the *present*' (2018: 94). But what if what Revelation consigns to the outside (at least in the homo- and transphobic interpretation of 22.15) were found to be on the inside all along, in the inmost inside location, indeed: the salvific body of its slain Messiah? This is the case, as we are about to see.

John's physical description of Jesus provides opportunity for strategic identification to sexually marginalized people of every race and ethnicity, not least those who share his skin colour and hair type – but not in modern translations of Revelation's Greek. 'I saw one like a son of man', says John, 'clothed with a long robe and with a golden sash across his *mastoi*' (1.13). *Mastoi* (singular: *mastos*) was the standard term in ancient Greek for female breasts. For example, in its more than two dozen occurrences in the Septuagint, the ancient Greek translation of the Hebrew scriptures, *mastos* invariably and unambiguously means '(female) breast', and *mastos* also has this meaning in its other two occurrences in the New Testament (Lk. 11.27; 23.29). For complicated reasons having to do with a Septuagintal mistranslation of Song 1.2, a text to which John is apparently alluding here (see Rainbow 2007: 250-2), the Jesus of Rev. 1.13 is endowed with female breasts.

Early commentators on Revelation, such as Caesarius of Arles (*Exposition on the Apocalypse* 1.13, homily 1) and Andrew of Caesarea (*Commentary on the Apocalypse* 1.13), acknowledged those breasts. For Andrew, for example, Jesus' breasts were maternal; they were 'the two Testaments, through which the faithful are nourished' (Constantinou 2011 trans.). The *mastoi* made their way into the Vulgate Latin translation of the New Testament as *mamillae*, a Latin term whose predominant meaning was likewise '(female) breasts'. Early English translators of the New Testament also made no attempt to hide the breasts. The King James Version of 1611 rendered the Greek phrase as 'girt about the paps with a golden girdle', and still earlier English translators also opted for 'paps' (Tyndale, 1534; Douay-Rheims, 1582; Bishop's Bible, 1595) or 'teats' (Wycliffe, 1395). Long before we get to the New King James Version (1979–82), however, which renders the Greek phrase as 'with a golden sash around his chest', Jesus' breasts have been fastidiously covered up – bound tightly, if you will – in every modern English translation and transformed into a manly chest.

What might be the contemporary significance of allowing Jesus' female breasts, his womanly cleavage, to remain visible under his golden sash, now become a brassiere? Potentially these breasts assume considerable weight within the context of a world Christianity in which the official position of many denominations towards LGBTQ+ persons is a highly contentious issue. In contemporary parlance, the Jesus held up for veneration in Rev. 1.13-16 is genderqueer. S/he – or, better, they – cannot be tidily contained within either category of the heteronormative gender binary. Purely in terms of anatomy, the Jesus of Rev. 1.13-16 is female. Other than their *mastoi*, no body part mentioned in their description (head, hair, eyes, feet, hand, mouth, face) functions as a marker of their biological sex. The presumed maleness of this Jesus rests purely on the masculine pronouns

John applies to them: 'his' (*autou*) and 'him' (*auton*). The anatomy John describes deconstructs the pronouns John uses for the person possessing the anatomy and vice versa.

That anatomy also stands in tension with John's initial description of the figure he beholds as 'one like a son of man' (*homoion huion anthrōpou* – 1.13). The contiguity of the terms 'son', 'man' and '(female) breasts' in the Greek of Rev. 1.13 disrupts gender-binary conceptions of the human. *Ho huios tou anthrōpou* in Rev. 1.13, 14.14 and elsewhere in the New Testament is rendered inclusively in the Common English Bible (2010–11) as 'the Human One'. But it is a differently gendered humanity that the risen Jesus manifests in Revelation's physical description of him. As such, Rev. 1.13 constitutes a powerful potential point of identification for trans, genderqueer, nonbinary or gender nonconforming persons of every kind within the Christian churches, on their fringes, or 'outside' (cf. Rev. 22.15) them altogether. Revelation 1.13 also deserves to stand alongside Jn 13.23 ('One of [Jesus'] disciples – the one whom Jesus loved – was reclining on his bosom [*kolpos*]') in queer-affirming scholarship on, and preaching from, the New Testament, a role it has yet to assume.

Jezebel thrown on a bed

Let us return to the seven letters that John has the risen Jesus dictate to the Christian assemblies of seven Asian cities (Rev. 2–3). These seven short letters share a similar structure. Each begins with the same introductory phrase ('Thus says [*tade legei*] … ', a formal mode of address that, among other things, could open royal decrees), followed by a poetic self-identification by the sender, Jesus ('[he] who holds the seven stars in his right hand' – 2.1; 'the first and the last' – 2.8; see also 2.12, 18; 3.1a, 7, 14). Then a report card follows, beginning with the words 'I know … " (e.g., 'I know your works, your toil, and your patient endurance' – 2.2; see also 2.9, 13, 19; 3.1b, 8, 15). Each church is either praised or censured for its attitudes and actions, which accounts for the principal portion of each letter (2.2-6, 9-10, 13-16, 19-25; 3.1b-4, 8-11, 15-20). Each then concludes with a call for attentiveness to the Holy Spirit ('listen to what the Spirit is saying') and a promise of divine rewards for those who 'conquer' – that is, who withstand the trials to which they will be subjected on account of their faith (2.7, 11, 17, 26-9; 3.5-6, 12-13, 21-2).

Of particular interest in the letters to the seven churches are cryptic references to 'the teaching of the Nicolaitans' (2.15; see also 2.6), 'the teaching of Balaam' (2.14) and the teaching of 'that woman Jezebel, who calls herself a prophet' (2.20). Nothing further is known about the Nicolaitans. References to them in subsequent second- and third-century Christian literature seem to depend ultimately on Revelation. Assumedly they were disciples of a teacher named Nicolaus, probably not the Nicolaus of Acts 6.5, although some ancient interpreters thought so (e.g., Irenaeus, *Against Heresies* 1.26.3; Clement of Alexandria, *Miscellanies* 2.20; 3.4). The phrase 'the teaching of Balaam' appears to be a synonym for the phrase 'the teaching of the Nicolaitans' (see Rev. 2.14-15). Furthermore, the content of Balaam's teaching is described in terms identical to that of Jezebel's teaching ('the teaching of Balaam, who taught Balak to put a stumbling block before the people of Israel, so that they would eat food sacrificed to idols and practice fornication' – 2:14; 'that woman Jezebel, who ... is teaching ... my servants to practice fornication and to eat food sacrificed to idols' – 2:20). John appears to be attacking a single group here rather than three different groups or individuals.

Balaam and Jezebel are both symbolic names. In Jewish scripture and tradition, they both epitomize error and wickedness (on Balaam, see, for example, Num. 31.16; Deut. 23.4-5; 2 Pet. 2.15-16; Philo, *Migration of Abraham* 113–14; *Life of Moses* 1.277, 294–9; Josephus, *Antiquities of the Jews* 4.129–30; on Jezebel, see, for example, 1 Kgs 21.25; 2 Kgs 9.7, 22; Josephus, *Antiquities of the Jews* 8.317–18). But John also has a specific contemporary in mind when he uses the name Jezebel. (This is probably not the case for Balaam, who seems in 2.14 to be purely a figure from the remote past.) Jezebel is a code name for a Christian prophet in the city of Thyatira – a female Nicolaitan prophet, to be precise. Furthermore, the charge of 'fornicating' (*porneusai*) that John levels against the Nicolaitans (2.14-15, 20-1) is likely symbolic. Fornication is a common metaphor for idolatry in the Jewish scriptures (e.g., Jer. 3.1-3, 6-9; Ezek. 16.26-9, 35-8; 23.1-21; Hos. 1.2; 4.10-13). John is really charging the Nicolaitans with what he sees as an idolatrous practice: 'eat[ing] food [that has been] sacrificed to idols' (Rev. 2.14, 20).

The Nicolaitans are best understood as Christ-followers who took a relaxed or pragmatic view of Christian accommodation to Roman civic society. Like their counterparts in the Corinthian church, and even Paul himself (1 Cor. 8.4, 7-8; 10.25-30), these Christ-followers have no problem with privately eating meat that has been sold in the marketplace after having been sacrificed in pagan temples, or with publicly eating meat in such socioreligious settings as the festivals associated with the imperial cult or the banquets hosted by trade guilds. The rival Christian prophet whom John contemptuously names 'Jezebel' appears to have been an assimilationist (Paul B. Duff's apt term for her [2001: 132]) who did not regard the Christian movement as fundamentally incompatible with the dominant culture. In contrast, John was a radical separatist for whom the Christian movement could have no common ground with that culture. John's call to Christ-followers to disassociate themselves from Roman culture later comes to succinct expression: 'Come out from her [i.e., Babylon/Rome], my people, so that you do not take part in her sins' (18.4). It is no accident that Revelation has frequently been a foundational text for Christian sects that have seen mainstream culture as irredeemably corrupt or compromised and as such have felt profoundly alienated from it.

John's separatism (and misogyny?) leads him to make some startling pronouncements on Jezebel. 'Look, I am throwing her on a bed [*Idou ballō autēn eis klinēn*]', John has his Jesus exclaim, 'and those who commit adultery with her I am throwing into great distress, unless they repent of her doings; and I will strike her children dead!' (2.21-23). The notion that the expression 'throw on a bed' is a Hebraism meaning 'cause to become ill' has been recycled by commentators for more than a century. In anglophone scholarship on Revelation it may be traced back to Henry Barclay Swete (1906: 43) and R. H. Charles (1920: 71–2), and hence to an exegetical era when the more obvious sexual connotation of the 'throwing on a bed' action, 'the Son of God' (2:18) being its subject, was all but unthinkable and certainly unarticulable. The anodyne interpretation of Rev. 2.22 has held on doggedly in scholarship on Revelation. As recently as 2014, to cite but one of a great many illustrations of its tenacity, Craig R. Koester translated the Greek phrase we have been considering as, 'See, I am going to put her to bed' (2014: 5, 299). Every other form of violence attributed to Jesus in Revelation can be contemplated with equanimity by commentators, whether his preparation of a horrid 'supper of God' composed of the flesh of his enemies (19.17-18), or his presiding over the eternal torture of those same enemies (14.9-11); but rape, it seems, is the step too far, the one form of violence that cannot be ascribed to Revelation's protagonist.

Since the latter decades of the twentieth century, all manner of previously unsayable things about any number of biblical texts have become utterable. Yet this particular thing proved particularly hard to say, even Tina Pippin

(1995: 193–5) stopping short from explicitly naming the action in Rev. 2.22 as rape while clearly implying that we are to see it as such. In time, however, a trickle of scholars began to acknowledge, even if only in passing, that punitive sexual violence seems to be implied in the phrase 'I am throwing her on a bed' (see esp. Marshall 2009: 21-22, 30, the most forthright grasping of the bull by the horns up to that point). For the bed onto which Jesus is throwing Jezebel is flanked by sexual activity on either side, in a veritable tangle of naked limbs: 'She doesn't wish to repent of her whoring [tēs porneias autēs]. Look, I am throwing her onto a bed, and those who commit adultery with her I am throwing into great distress' (2.21-2). The immediate context thus invites the conclusion that the punishment being visited on Jezebel is itself sexual, a repaying in kind appropriate to the nature of her transgression.

The lex talionis principle is later articulated explicitly in relation to Babylon: 'Render to her as she herself has rendered, and repay her double for her deeds …. As she glorified herself and lived luxuriously, so give her a like measure of torment and grief' (18.6-7). In the previous scene, this revenge fantasy had taken an explicitly sexual form: 'And the ten horns that you saw, they and the beast will hate the whore; they will make her desolate and naked; they will devour her flesh and burn her up with fire' (17.16, a verse we ponder further below). And why do they do these horrific things to her? 'For [gar] God has put it into their hearts' (17.17). The indirect agency of God in 17.16-17 in administering a sexualized punishment to 'the great whore' (17.1; 19.2) obliquely mirrors the more direct agency of the Son of God in 2.22 in administering a sexualized punishment to Jezebel for her 'whoring'.

This parallel is not accidental. Jezebel exists in an intimate relationship with Revelation's other 'wicked woman', who is 'Babylon the great, mother of whores and of earth's abominations' (17.5). In John's mind, Babylon, as imperial Rome, represents the threat from outside to the Christian assemblies to whom he is writing, notably the threat of persecution ('And I saw that the woman was drunk with the blood of the saints and the blood of the witnesses to Jesus' – 17:6), whereas Jezebel represents the threat from within, the threat of Christian assimilation to Roman culture. That double threat is symbolized, for John, by two sexualized women. And the overcoming of the threat is symbolized by two startling instances of sexual violence, Jezebel raped on a bed by none other than the risen Jesus himself (2.22), and Babylon stripped, devoured and burned by the beast and its minions while God looks on approvingly (17.16-17).

A dead elephant in the divine throne room

In Rev. 4.1-2, the action shifts abrupt to the heavenly throne room ('There in heaven a door stood open! And the … voice … said, "Come up here"'), so called because its central feature is 'the one seated on the throne', an image for God used twelve times in Revelation (4.2, 9-10 [twice]; 5.1, 7, 13; 6.16; 7.10, 15; 19.4; 20.11; 21.5), yet another of the book's 'hidden' numbers of significance. As in the Jewish scriptures (e.g., 1 Kgs 22.19; Job 1.6; Dan. 7.9-10; see also *1 Enoch* 14.18-22; *Apocalypse of Abraham* 18.3-14), the god of Israel is conceived in Revelation on the model of an earthly monarch surrounded by courtiers and other attendants, but, unlike any earthly monarch, is seated above the dome of the sky (see esp. Isa. 40.22; also Exod. 24.9-10; Job 22.12-14; Ps. 11.4; Isa. 64.1; Ezek. 1.22, 26). The heavenly throne room doubles as a heavenly temple in Revelation, both because it is a sacrificial space, as we shall see (cf. Heb. 4.14-16; 8.1-2), and because it is the scene of an eternal liturgy (Rev. 4.8-11). Eternal life in Revelation, whether for angels and other heavenly beings or for human beings, is, indeed, an eternal worship service (see esp. 7.15; 22.3-4). In other words, the place in Revelation from which absolute power is exercised is also the place in which absolute power is worshipped.

The barely describable being who is seated on Revelation's throne (4.2-6) clutches a scroll that has been 'sealed with seven seals' (5.1). As the ensuing narrative indicates, this scroll is an eschatological timetable. The successive breaking of its seals triggers the divinely preordained sequence of events that inaugurates the end of history. Jesus, whom we last encountered as 'one like a son of man' (1.13), now reappears to open the scroll (5.2-6). He has, however, shed his humanoid form. Now he is a lamb (*arnion*), and in that animal form he will remain through most of the rest of Revelation.

It is really as a zoomorphic entity, an animal-bodied being, that the Jesus of Rev. 5ff. has traditionally been imagined. When, in the Gospel of John, the approaching Jesus is identified by John the Baptist as 'the lamb of God [*ho amnos tou theou*] who takes away the sin of the world' (1.29; see also 1.36; Acts 8.32; 1 Cor. 5.7; 1 Pet. 1.18-19) exceedingly few readers or hearers have imagined a woolly four-legged mammal trotting along the banks of the Jordan to meet with the Baptist. But a quadrupedal mammal is precisely what the Christian imagination, not least the artistic imagination (see Kovacs and Rowland 2004: 74–5; O'Hear and O'Hear 2015: 52–69), has tended overwhelmingly to visualize standing in Revelation's heavenly throne room and proceeding through most of the ensuing narrative. This is a transmutation of Jesus of Nazareth that, all told, is more remarkable and more radical even than his appearance in Revelation 1 as an angelic, female-breasted being. It is also a christological image with much relevance for ecological reflection on Revelation, as we shall later see.

The description of the Lamb in the heavenly throne room has it 'standing as if it had been slaughtered' (*hestēkos hōs esphagmenon* – 5.6), a symbolic reference to Jesus' crucifixion interpreted primarily as a sacrifice for sin (see esp. 1.5: '[Jesus] freed us from our sins by his blood'; see also 5.9; 7.14; 12.10-11; 19.13; Lev. 14.10-32), even if other layers of meaning may also be plausibly ascribed to the image. Scholars of Revelation typically mull over the question of which sacrificial texts in the Hebrew Bible are or are not evoked by Revelation's slain Lamb (e.g., Aune 1997: 367–73; Johns 2003: 22–39; Koester 2014: 376–7) but fail to grapple with more fundamental and more relevant issues related to animal sacrifice as such.

The main business of ancient temples was the ritual slaughter of animals, gods being almost universally conceived as beings whose favour depended on the spilling of blood. As such, animal sacrifice was the central institution of most ancient religions, not least those of the Roman world, ranging from the official religion of the Roman state to provincial religions such as Judaism. The author of the Letter to the Hebrews states succinctly (and does not contest) the ancient Israelite theology of sacrifice as it pertains to guilt and sin: 'Without the shedding of blood there is no [divine] forgiveness of sins' (9.22; see further Lev. 4.1–6.7; 6.24-30; 7.1-10, and esp. 17.11).

Ancient sacrificial religions, like the cultures out of which they emerged – and like most cultures down through the ages, up to and including mainstream US culture – operated on the premise that slaughtering a nonhuman animal does not constitute murder. The sacrificial lamb presented to us in Rev. 5, however, is, implicitly, an unjustly killed animal. To be sure, the reason that the slaughter of this particular lamb was a heinous crime, one sufficient to cause 'all the tribes of the earth [to] wail' (1.7), is that this lamb, in addition to its explicit narrative identity as a nonhuman mammal, also possesses an implicit human identity, that of the crucified man Jesus of Nazareth. And yet we should not move too swiftly from the lamb to the man. Revelation's predominant image for the human being Jesus of Nazareth is a nonhuman animal, as we have seen. As such, Revelation blurs the sharp, clearly defined conceptual line that separated human from nonhuman animals in the ancient world, enabling, among other things, the existence of sacrificial religions; and that blurs the even sharper line dividing human from nonhuman animals in our own era, enabling, through the emergence of the modern industrial slaughterhouse, mass nonmurder of nonhuman animals on a scale never before seen. Revelation 5 presents us with a spectacle that has become more, not less, relevant with the passage of time: the ethical paradox of a sacrificial animal whose slaughter constitutes an unlawful killing.

Can Revelation be said, then, to engage in a critique of the sacrificial system, akin to those mounted by Lucian, Porphyry and other ancient pagan critics of animal sacrifice (see Gilhus 2006: 138–60 for their arguments)? Not quite. Revelation subtly deconstructs the ethical logic of ancient sacrifice, as we have seen, and in ways that are relevant for contemporary theological reflection on human interaction with nonhuman animals. But Revelation also relies on the sacrificial logic it undercuts. That the slaughter of the particular animal presented to us in Rev. 5 was an ethically reprehensible act, an unjust killing, does not make it a purely destructive act, or even an ineffective sacrifice. On the contrary, Revelation represents this act of bloodshed as not only the pivotal moment in the history of salvation but the most successful sacrifice ever performed. When the Lamb has taken the eschatological scroll 'from the right hand of the one who was seated on the throne' (5.7), the four living creatures and the twenty-four elders around the throne commence a hymn of praise, lauding the Lamb's worthiness to receive the scroll and open its seals, a hymn that the 'myriads of myriads' of angels in heaven also take up, and eventually every creature 'on earth and under the earth and in the sea' (5.8-14). What makes the Lamb worthy of such honour? The fact that it was the sacrificial victim in the ultimate sacrifice: 'You are worthy ..., for you were slaughtered and by your blood you ransomed [*ēgorasas*] for God saints from every tribe and language and people and nation' (5.9; cf. 14.3b; 1 Cor. 6.20; 7.23; Heb. 9.11-14, 24-6; 1 Pet. 1.18-19).

Undisturbed and unquestioned in Revelation, then, are the efficacy and indispensability of the ancient sacrificial machine. Far from declaring the machine obsolete, Revelation implicitly insists, not only that the machine still works, but that it works better, with more spectacular success, than it has ever worked before. John will later be confronted with 'a great multitude that no one could count, from every nation, from all tribes and peoples and languages, standing before the throne and before the Lamb, robed in white', and will be told: 'These are they who have ... washed their robes in the blood of the Lamb' (7.9, 14; see also 12.11). Earlier John himself had exulted: 'To him who loves us and freed us from our sins by his blood, ... be glory and dominion forever and ever!' (1.5b). For the author of Revelation as for the author of Hebrews, there can be no divine forgiveness of sins 'without the shedding of blood' (Heb. 9.22). The God of Revelation, like the God of too many other biblical books to list, and like the gods of almost every known ancient religion, is a God who, for reasons that ultimately remain obscure, demands blood, a God whose favour depends on the spilling of blood – indeed, of innocent blood, whether that of a nonhuman animal or an unjustly executed human being. Arguably, this is the most sizeable (dead) elephant in the room of biblical scholarship, most of all New Testament scholarship, the most consequential theological and ethical question almost never discussed by biblical scholars.

The Jewish apocalypse of John

What more may be said about Revelation's relations to Judaism? Much that has seldom been said, as we are about to see. Especially illuminating in this regard is Rev. 7.1-7. This narrative unit, situated between the breaking of the sixth and seventh seals, is the first of Revelation's so-called interludes or digressions – terms that should not, however, be taken to imply that such material is of secondary importance. Revelation 7.1-17 interrupts the seal-opening sequence to introduce two seemingly disparate groups: 144,000 'servants [literally, "slaves": *douloi*] of … God' marked 'with a seal on their foreheads' (7.3; cf. Ezek. 9.4) and 'a great multitude that no one could count' (Rev. 7.9). This great multitude has undergone 'the great ordeal' (*hē thlipsis hē megalē* – 7.14). The more famous English translation of this Greek phrase is 'the great tribulation' (KJV), and it is ordinarily understood to be a reference to mass, martyr-making persecution. But the divine protection signalled by their earlier 'sealing' (7.2-4) has enabled the great multitude to pass through the ordeal without denying Jesus (cf. 2.13; 3.10).

That the 144,000 and the great multitude are best seen, not as two separate groups, but rather as a single group focused from two different angles, has long (see, for example, Charles 1920, I,199) been a common argument in critical scholarship on Revelation. The implications of this position, however, for John's relations to Judaism have seldom if ever been articulated. First, some preliminary observations. The number 144,000 is a symbolic one here rather than a literal one, most especially if the 144,000 is to be equated with the 'great multitude that no one could count' (7.9). Underlying the symbolic import of the number 144,000 is the number twelve, as we saw earlier: 12,000 people are 'sealed' with 'the seal of the living God' from each of the twelve tribes of Israel (7.2-8). Twelve acquires its primary significance in Revelation from being at once the number of the twelve tribes and the number of the twelve apostles. The only other explicit mention of the twelve tribes in Revelation comes at the climax of the book, the description of the new Jerusalem that descends from heaven to earth. We are told that the city has twelve gates, 'and on the gates are inscribed the names of the twelve tribes of the Israelites' (21.12). The city also has twelve foundations, 'and on them are the twelve names of the twelve apostles of the Lamb' (21.14). As we shall later see, the city is itself an elaborate metaphor for the people of God. The Jewish people of God? The Christian people of God? Revelation muddies that distinction, nowhere more thoroughly than in the description of the 144,000 'sealed out of every tribe of the people of Israel' that, viewed from a different angle, abruptly becomes 'a great multitude … from every nation, from all tribes and peoples and languages' (7.4, 9). How is this dual focus possible?

The 144,000 are almost certainly not to be identified as ethnic Jews; their juxtaposition with the great multitude makes that highly unlikely. By the same token, however, within Revelation's implied ethnic logic, the great multitude is almost certainly not to be identified as Christians as distinct from Jews (see Marshall 2001: 18). Within the socioreligious world of Revelation, 'Christianity' has not yet parted from 'Judaism', has not yet been conceived even as separate from it, much less as superseding it. Implicitly, the 144,000/great multitude is made up of Gentile as well as Jewish Christ-followers. John's view of the relationship of Gentile Christ-followers to Judaism likely parallels that of Paul. For Paul, the Gentile church is incorporated into Israel, 'grafted' into the Jewish ancestral tree through faith in Jesus Messiah (Rom. 11.13-24), so as to become a beneficiary of the covenant privileges originally bestowed on Israel and to share in the blessings of salvation to which Israel alone was heir (9.4-5). These and other such tenets of 'the new perspective on Paul' have revolutionized Pauline scholarship. A corresponding transformation of the scholarly understanding of Revelation's relations to Judaism, however – a 'new perspective on Revelation'? – despite promising beginnings, has never quite taken off (Frankfurter 2001, 2011 and Marshall 2001, 2007 have been foundational to this endeavour, and Emanuel 2020 is its most significant recent product).

What might be the broad contours of a new perspective on Revelation? As the 144,000/great multitude amalgam implies, John sees followers of Jesus Messiah as 'true Jews', whether they are ethnically Jewish or not – provided, as we shall see, that they strictly observe the halakhic ordinances stemming from the Torah and designed to regulate daily existence. (This is where John and Paul would have parted company; see Frankfurter 2001: 403, 412ff.; Marshall 2001: 142–3.) In the letters to the churches in Smyrna and Philadelphia, John's Jesus bitterly derides ethnic Jews who, apparently, denounce Christ-followers to the civic authorities (see 2.9-10): '[They] say that they are Jews and are not, but are a synagogue of Satan' (2.9; see also 3.9). The internal evidence of Revelation indicates overwhelmingly that John himself is a Christ-confessing Jew, beginning with the fact that his prose is so deeply saturated with the phrases and thought patterns of the Jewish scriptures; and his grammar and syntax are so often Hebrew or Aramaic rather than Greek, causing one scholar, as we noted earlier, to argue compellingly that John's diction is the 'pidginized "ghetto Greek"' of a diasporic Jew (Callahan 1995: 454). More precisely, the internal evidence suggests that John is a halakhically observant Christ-confessing Jew; for purity is a central preoccupation in Revelation (see Frankfurter 2001: 410–12; Marshall 2001: 155–62; Stenström 2009), as in so many other expressions of ancient Judaism.

The symbolic lines of separation in Revelation run consistently between the pure and the impure. Those who follow the Lamb are a community of priests (1.6; 5.10; 20.6; cf. 3.12a), and as such custodians of purity. They 'have not been defiled/made dirty [*ouk emolynthēsan*] with women' (14.4) and are therefore 'unblemished' (*amōmoi* – 14.5). 'Jezebel' and her followers, in contrast, perform impure acts – 'fornication', in Revelation's parlance – eating meat that has been sacrificed to idols (2.20; see also 2.14, 21). The woman 'Babylon', for her part, not only abandons herself to defiling sexual activity – her cup contains 'the impurities/pollutions of her prostitution/fornication [*ta akatharta tēs porneias autēs*]' (17.4) – but she even drinks blood (17.6; cf. 16.6; 18.6), 'the ultimate impurity' (Marshall 2009: 29). When she mutates into a city, Babylon is home to demons and 'every unclean [*akathartou*] spirit' and 'every unclean and loathsome [*akathartou kai memisēmenou*] bird' (and animal, in some ancient manuscripts; 18.2). In contrast, nothing 'unclean/profane' (*koinon*) shall enter the 'holy city' (21.27; cf. 22.15). Its conspicuous cubic structure (21.16) evokes the inner sanctuary of Solomon's temple (1 Kgs 6.20), the 'most holy place' (1 Kgs 6.16), and hence the place most inimical to impurity.

In short, 'Revelation provides a textbook example of how "purity" can structure a symbolic universe' (Stenström 2009: 49). Consonant with this preoccupation, and returning to the scene with which we began, the 'great multitude ... from every nation' of Rev. 7.9, which is simultaneously the 144,000 'sealed out of every tribe of the people of Israel' (7.4), have 'washed their robes and made them white' in the cleansing blood of the sacrificial Lamb (7.14) and now 'worship [God] day and night within his temple' (7.15). Although it is not yet generally recognized as such, Revelation deserves to stand alongside the Gospel of Matthew as the New Testament text that most fully preserves the Christ-confessing Judaism that Gentile Christianity would eventually erase, particularly after the fourth century when the latter would merge seamlessly with the Roman Empire that Revelation was resisting in the first century.

Just vengeance?

Let's double back to Rev. 6.1–8.2, the second of the major series of seven that propel Revelation's plot, the Lamb breaking the seven seals on his scroll one by one. The opening of the first four seals (6.1-8) unleashes the chaos of war and its consequences, as we saw. The opening of the fifth seal (6.9-11) elicits Revelation's first reference to the mass killing of Christ-followers (see also 7.9, 13-14; 16.5-6; 17.6; 20.4). Indeed, the same verb, *sphazō*, 'slaughter' is used for them ('I saw under the altar the souls of those who had been slaughtered [*esphagmenōn*] for the word of God and for the testimony they had given' – 6.9) as was used earlier for the Lamb ('I saw between the throne and the four living creatures ... a Lamb standing as if it had been slaughtered [*esphagmenon*]' – 5.6). If Jesus was animalized by reason of his slaughter, so too, apparently, were those whose testimony (*martyria*) to him also resulted in violent death; for they are assembled under the heavenly altar before God's throne (see 8.3) and altars were places of animal sacrifice in antiquity. According to Leviticus, moreover, the blood of sacrificed animals is to be poured out at the base of the altar (4.7, 18, 25, etc.), which is precisely where the 'souls' (*psychai*) of the slaughtered huddle.

Like the Lamb's slaughter, too, the slaughter of the Lamb's followers is marked as an unjust killing. The martyrs not only cry out for justice, but they also cry out for vengeance: 'Sovereign Lord, holy and true, how long will it be before you judge and avenge [*krineis kai ekdikeis*] our blood on the inhabitants of the earth?' (6.10; cf. *4 Ezra* 4.33-7). Many mainstream commentators on Revelation squirm at the notion that the martyrs are demanding vengeance from God no less than justice – justice in the form of vengeance – and are being assured that they will receive it in due course (Rev. 6.11), as indeed they do; for we later read: 'He [God] has judged [*ekrinen*] the great whore ... and he has avenged [*exedikēsen*] on her the blood of his servants' (19.2; see also 16.4-7). Such squeamishness is understandable: a vengeful God, bristling with 'wrath' (see 6.16-17; 11.18; 14.10, 19; 15.1; 16.1, 19; 19.15), might be thought to exemplify biblical anthropomorphism (projecting onto the deity human, all too human, traits) at its least palatable.

Alternatively, is a wrathful God – a vengeful God, even – possessed of a human rage for justice precisely what is needed in the face of inhuman injustice? Certain liberationist exegetes of Revelation have said or implied as much, none more searingly than Allan Boesak (1987: 68–70), whose words, written from within the bestial belly of the South African apartheid regime, are worth quoting at length:

> The cry 'How long, Lord?' has been the cry of the suffering faithful down through the ages .... It is a cry of pain and anguish; it is a cry of protest. It is also a cry of hope that God will prove to be the Mighty One, the help of the helpless .... At the moment of detention; in the long dark hours of incarceration; as the footsteps of your interrogators come down the passage to your cell; above the harsh voices and the scornful laugh; through the blows of fists on tender flesh, the blinding pain of electric shocks; through the hazy, bloody mist of unwanted tears ... – the words are shouted or whispered: 'How long, Lord?' ... It is a cry black South Africans who find their help in Yahweh have been uttering for a long time. They have lived under racist colonial oppression for almost three and a half centuries, and under the particularly vicious form of racism called apartheid for nearly four decades .... During recent years there has hardly been a place where the police and the army have not wantonly murdered our children, piling atrocity upon atrocity for the sake of the preservation of apartheid and white privilege. And as they go from funeral to funeral, burying yet another victim of law and order or yet another killed by government-protected death squads, the cry continues to rise to heaven: 'How long, Lord?' How long before this illegitimate power is removed? How long before the blood of our children is avenged?

As it happens, the cry for justice and vengeance from the martyrs in Revelation comes immediately after its first indication that the 'illegitimate power' of the Roman Empire is about to be removed; for prior to John's vision of the souls under the altar, Revelation's four horsemen have ridden forth (6.1-8).

The first rider, in particular, the one on the white horse bearing a bow and wearing a crown, has been an object of speculation through the ages, and much of that speculation implicitly makes the rider a vehicle of vengeance.

The interpretation of the figure as Christ himself, returning in glory, may be traced back to the third century and Victorinus of Pettau (*Commentary on the Apocalypse* 6.1-2). Certain modern interpreters, however, have instead seen the bow-wielding rider on the white horse as representing the Parthian threat to Rome. The Parthians were a Persian people whose most formidable military asset was their mounted archers. The Parthians built up an empire that preceded Rome's and coexisted alongside it on its eastern border.

Revelation also seems to evoke the Parthian threat to Rome in 9.13-19, which mentions 'the great river Euphrates', the boundary between the two empires, and describes a vast demonic cavalry with immense destructive power that is destined to be unleashed, arguably from the Parthian side of the river. The detail of the cavalry horses having their 'power … in their mouths and in their tails' (9.19) has sometimes been read as a reference to 'the Parthian shot', the Parthian cavalry's tactic of shooting one volley of arrows over their horses' heads as they charged and a second volley over their horses' tails as they retreated. Thundering Parthian hooves have also been heard in 16.12, which describes 'the great river Euphrates' being 'dried up in order to prepare the way for the kings from the east'. But when John was writing his apocalypse, Parthia was by no means a future threat only. The Roman legions had already suffered three defeats at the hands of the Parthians, most notably at Rhandia in western Armenia in 62 CE, a particularly shaming rout for Rome and its then Emperor Nero, one of Revelation's prime villains, as we have seen.

Roll into all of this the myth of Nero *redivivus*, which, as we also saw, had Nero escaping execution, fleeing to the east and awaiting the day when he would return to Rome at the head of a Parthian horde to wreak vengeance on it. Nero is a brooding if unnamed presence in Revelation, balefully peering out from behind its pages, and not only in 13.3 and 13.18, the coded statements about the beast's 'mortal wound' and its 'number' that we deciphered earlier. Nero is also often thought to be lurking behind 9.11 as well, a verse that identifies the commander of the Parthian-evoking demon cavalry as Apollyon. Towards the end of his reign, Nero identified himself publicly and insistently with the god Apollo, as ancient sources abundantly testify (see Champlin 2003: 112–44). And what of 17.6, the woman Babylon's worse-than-rape? She is stripped, ravaged, burned and devoured. She symbolizes 'the great city' (17.18), Rome. But those who enact the sexualized annihilation of Babylon are led by 'the beast [who] hate[s] the whore' (17.16; cf. 17.12-13); and the beast, as we have seen, is, among other things and above all, Nero (13:18).

What, then, should we conclude? That a demonic Nero sits at the head of a fiendish Parthian army in Revelation, an unstoppable mounted horde that rampages periodically across its pages, an instrument of divine judgement and wrath unleashed against Rome, the thought of which fills John's heart with vengeful joy? Even if we put the brakes on such speculation, tying the Parthians less specifically to these texts (they were not the only mounted archers on Rome's frontiers, after all), a non-Roman military force is evoked nonetheless, since the Romans themselves did not deploy mounted archers until the early second century CE (Koester 2014: 394–95), and so the basic elements of John's revenge fantasy remain undisturbed. Periodically in Revelation, John is obliquely conjuring up for his implied, Rome-hating audience, the welcome spectre of an earthly army that, even before Jesus returns at the head of his own heavenly cavalry (19.11-14), will be equipped to stand toe to toe with the Romans, and even to defeat the Romans, because John's God wills it, whether or not that anti-Roman military power be conceived as generic tribal forces from beyond Rome's borders or as Parthian forces specifically. In other words, John of Patmos, writing as a member of a conquered people, is gleefully brandishing the Parthian threat, or the more general 'barbarian' threat, in the face of Roman imperialism.

Later in the book, in one of its climactic scenes, the fall of Babylon (John's code word for Rome, as we know) is proleptically and exultantly enacted in loving detail (18.1–19.5) – again, before Jesus has returned. John is thoroughly vague about the causes of Rome's demise. To ask whether the agents of Babylon/Rome's eschatological destruction are purely supernatural or merely human would be to impose a distinction on Revelation's narrative world that it refuses at every turn. The agents of this divinely willed – and thoroughly vengeful (19.2; see also 18.6-8) – destruction are human forces in the grip of supernatural powers. And John seeks to activate these agents in and through his prophetic vision. The power of John's prophetic/proleptic vision inheres in its capacity to answer, again and again, the cries for justice, for vengeance – for just vengeance – that oppressed people have uttered through the ages, raising their voices in chorus with those of the slaughtered ones under the heavenly altar (6.9), people like the black South Africans under apartheid on whose behalf Allen Boesak implored: '"How long, Lord?" How long before this illegitimate power is removed? How long before the blood of our children is avenged?' (1987: 70).

What of Armageddon? How does it fit into Revelation's overall scenario of cathartic, militarized, divine vengeance? Let us return to the banks of the Euphrates, making sure to stand well back. The sixth angel has just poured out his bowl 'full of the wrath of God' (15.7) on the river, causing it to dry up 'in order to prepare the way for the kings from the east' (16.12). We are also shown 'three foul spirits like frogs coming from the mouth of the dragon [who is Satan], from the mouth of the [sea] beast, and from the mouth of the false prophet [who is the land beast]' (16.13). This is John's grotesque reworking of the plague of frogs from the Exodus narrative (Exod. 8.1-7). The mundane frogs of that plague, now become 'demonic spirits' (Rev. 16.14), are assigned the task of assembling the kings of the earth for the battle of Harmagedon (16.16), better known as Armageddon, another of Revelation's most iconic images. Ironically, however, this war that, in the popular imagination, is the war to end all wars, receives only an ephemeral mention in Revelation. The battle is not described in the chapter in which it is named. Most likely, it is the same battle later described in 19.19-21 and/or 20.7-10, but the name Harmagedon does not occur again after 16.16.

The staging area for the undescribed battle of 16.14, 16 is a nonexistent mountain. Harmagedon is usually thought to be a transliteration of *har-mĕgiddô(n)*, Hebrew for 'mountain of Megiddo'. Geographically and scripturally, Megiddo is both a plain and a city in northern Israel, but not a mountain. This has led to the recurrent scholarly suggestion that Harmagedon may instead be a transliteration of '*îr-mĕgiddô(n)*, Hebrew for 'city of Megiddo'. Either way, Megiddo was associated with important battles between Israel and its enemies (Judg. 5.19; 2 Kgs 23.29-30; 2 Chron. 35.22; see also Zech. 12.11). Israel has been realigned in Revelation around the person whom John deems to be Israel's Messiah (see esp. 7.4; 14.1) and Israel's enemies have been supernaturalized, but the element of warfare remains constant. Revelation is a book of war.

The principal combatant in the first of Revelation's climactic battles, 19.11-21, is Jesus Messiah himself, as we shall see, and his principal adversary is the beast, which is to say Rome. What has Jesus been up to since he unsealed the seven seals of the heavenly scroll, a task that ended in 8.1? In answering that question, we are brought up against the fact that Revelation's plot does not unfold in a linear or sequential fashion – something Victorinus already noticed in the third century (*Commentary on the Apocalypse* 8.2). Descriptions of the end of the age are not confined to the end of the book but are woven through it, and there are flashbacks as well to events that predate its first chapter.

An eclipse of the son

One such flashback is Jesus' birth, and Revelation's retelling of it is as different as can possibly be imagined from the tellings found in Matthew's and Luke's infancy narratives. Revelation repackages the birth of a peasant child to a peasant mother (the historical substratum of the event, which Luke, at least, retains: see Lk. 2.6-7) as a full-fledged myth enacted on a cosmic scale. 'The woman clothed with the sun' of Rev. 12.1, 'with the moon under her feet, and on her head a crown of twelve stars', is a composite figure, a polyvalent symbol. She is Mary because she is the mother of the Messiah (12.2, 5a). She is the church because her persecuted 'children [are] those who keep the commandments of God and hold the testimony of Jesus' (12.17). She is Zion, the holy city of Jerusalem, who, in the poetic phrases of Isaiah, labours and delivers her children, God acting as midwife, and nurtures them lovingly (Isa. 66.7-12). More even than Zion, she is Israel because her crown of twelve stars (Rev. 12.1) represents Israel's twelve tribes (cf. 7.4-8; 21.12) and because she escapes into the wilderness on eagles' wings (12.14), as Israel did earlier (Exod. 19.1-4). She is Eve because she is locked in a deadly struggle with the serpent (Gen. 3.14-15; Rev. 12.4b, 13-19) who, in Revelation, is also the dragon and Satan (12.9; 20.2). But she is also the pagan Queen of Heaven. The twelve stars in her crown also represent the twelve signs of the Zodiac. In addition, she is the goddess Leto who, pregnant with Apollo, son of the supreme god Zeus, flees the dragon Python in ancient Greek mythology. Roman imperial propaganda made use of elements of this myth, assigning certain emperors, most notably Augustus, the role of Apollo in it. In John's retooling of the myth, the Roman emperor is displaced by an imperial Christ destined 'to rule all the nations with a rod of iron' (12.5a; cf. Ps. 2.7-9; Rev. 11.15).

The woman clothed with the sun is the most prominent female character in Revelation after the woman Babylon, but she is no less stereotypical. Her capacity to bear children is her defining trait, her raison d'être as a character. Her glory is a reflection of her son's glory; she is important because he is important. She is without a name. And she does not have a single line – indeed, a single word – to utter. The only sounds ascribed to her are inarticulate cries of pain: 'She was … crying out … in the agony of giving birth' (12.2). For Tina Pippin, she is 'a goddess subdued, tamed', thoroughly under male control (2005: 136). And yet, she *is* a goddess nonetheless, as Catherine Keller has insisted (1996: 64–6). And goddesses, even mute goddesses, are in exceedingly short supply in the New Testament canon and in Christianity generally. And so we should make the most of her.

Mexican Christians have certainly made the most of her. Revelation 12.1 is the principal source of the iconography for the Virgin of Guadalupe, the preeminent Mexican representation of the mother of Jesus. The image of the Virgin miraculously emblazoned (so her legend goes) on the outer garment of Aztec convert Juan Diego Cuauhtlatoatzin on 12 December 1531 was of a woman radiating sunrays from her entire body, wearing a twelve-point crown, and standing on a crescent moon. The image, certain of whose details also evoked the indigenous deities of the Mesoamerican peoples (not least the Aztec star goddess Citlalicue), now hangs in the Basílica de Nuestra Señora de Guadalupe in Mexico City, the most visited Roman Catholic pilgrimage site in the world.

Miguel Sánchez, author of *Imagen de la Virgen María* (1648), the first published account of Juan Diego's vision, interpreted the indigenous features of the icon as signifying that the Spanish conquest and assimilation of the 'New World' had been accomplished through the power and patronage of the Virgin Mary. During the Mexican revolt against Spanish rule, however, launched in earnest in 1810, the battle cry was 'Death to the Spaniards and long live the Virgin of Guadalupe' and the rebel forces carried banners bearing the image of the Virgin. As even these few details suggest, the history of this celebrated icon traversed a circuitous path from being an expression of imperialism to being an anti-imperial emblem – as did the ancient history of the goddess Leto, mother of Apollo, in her own passage from being a figure of Roman imperial propaganda to being recast by the author of Revelation to become the mother of the hero of his anti-Roman apocalypse, while still bearing the marks of her indigenous pagan origins (see further D. Sánchez 2008: 47–82). In the convoluted reception history of Revelation 12, as it passes through Mexican colonial and national history, the repressed goddess (Greek and then Aztec) makes a triumphant return, and the mother comes to eclipse the son.

Back in the book of Revelation, however, the son shows no signs of fading into the background, and after Revelation 12 his adversaries are symbolized not only as beastly but as womanly besides.

Loathing (while loving) Babylon

Revelation 14.1-5 reintroduces the Lamb and the 144,000 'slaves [*douloi*] of God' who 'have been redeemed from the earth' (7.3-4; 14.3b). The 144,000 are now said to be those 'who have not defiled themselves with women [*meta gynaikōn ouk emolynthēsan*], for they are virgins' (14.4). To explain this statement (and short circuit its shock value), commentators have routinely appealed, for almost a century now, to ancient texts where sexual abstinence is a prerequisite for participation in 'holy war' against the perceived enemies of Yahweh (e.g., Deut. 23.9-10; 1 Sam. 21.5; 2 Sam. 11.11; 1QM [= the Dead Sea scroll known as the War Scroll] 7.3-6). The gender ideology that comes to expression in Rev. 14.4a is deeply problematic nonetheless as has been frequently argued ever since feminist sensibilities took root in Revelation scholarship – and not only because the Lamb's full cohort, the 144,000 introduced in 7.1-8 as the entire company of the redeemed, is implicitly represented as male in this statement, but because the female represents impurity in it. It is hardly coincidental that Revelation's ultimate symbol for impurity, the woman Babylon, makes her first appearance in the book almost immediately after this scene (see 14.8).

Of course, Babylon also symbolizes Rome in Revelation, and Revelation is the most unequivocal example of anti-imperial resistance literature in the New Testament. This is an enormously important feature of Revelation, and one that classic liberation theology and hermeneutics have long held up as inspiration for contemporary struggles against imperial or neo-imperial oppression, as we noted earlier. When, however, a feminist lens is brought to bear on Revelation in tandem with the liberationist lens, disquieting questions arise about Revelation's anti-imperial rhetoric.

Simply put, Revelation's attack on Rome is conducted through the medium of gender. Imperial Rome is represented in Revelation not just as a beast, but as a woman (14.8; 17.1-6; 18.3-8; 19.1-2). This should not surprise us. 'Babylon', the contemptuous code name hurled at Rome in Revelation, is the prototypical evil empire in the Hebrew Bible where it is already personified as female ('Sit in the dust, virgin daughter Babylon! Sit on the ground without a throne …!' – Isa. 47.1; see further 47.2-15; Jer. 50.9-15; Zech. 2.7). Note, however, that the epithet 'whore' (Hebrew: *zānāh*; Greek: *pornē*) is never levelled at Babylon in the Jewish scriptures or in any other extant Jewish source prior to Revelation. That sexual slur, slung at Babylon/ Rome (Rev. 17.1, 5, 15-16; 19.2), is all John's own.

The roots of John's female personification of Rome do not, however, descend purely into the Jewish scriptures. In representing Rome as a woman, John also took his inspiration from Roman imperial propaganda. Rome was already represented as female in the cult of the goddess Roma, a cult with a long history and high visibility in the province of Asia. A temple to *Thea Rhōmē*, the goddess Roma, had stood at Smyrna, one of Revelation's seven cities, since 195 BCE, as we saw earlier, the first-known temple to Roma in the ancient world. The Romaia, a lavish series of religious rituals, athletic contests and other public spectacles designed to honour the goddess, were conducted not only in Smyrna, but also in Ephesus, Sardis, Pergamum and Thyatira, another four of Revelation's seven cities. A temple dedicated to Roma and Divus Julius (the deified Julius Caesar), and another temple dedicated to Roma and Augustus, also stood in Ephesus. In other words, the goddess Roma would have been a figure with whom John's target audience would have been intimately familiar. Given that visual representations of Rome as a woman would have been commonplace in the cities to whose Christian assemblies Revelation is addressed, it is tempting to view 'Babylon the great, mother of whores and of earth's abominations' (Rev. 17.5) as John's parody of the goddess Roma (see Beauvery 1983: 243–60; Aune 1998b: 919–28). In the manner of a modern political cartoonist, John depicts Roma, the noble female personification of Roman might and virtue, as a shameless, out-of-control prostitute who has had too much to drink and whose antics and excesses invite derisive laughter from Revelation's audience (see Emanuel 2020: 126–66 passim).

Why is Rome represented as a sex worker in Revelation? Recall that the *seductiveness* of Roman culture is seen by John as an acute problem for the Christian assemblies in the cities of Roman Asia. John's stance on Christian participation in the socioreligious civic life of Roman Asia, not least its imperial cult, is sternly anti-assimilationist or separatist ('Come out of her, my people' – 18.4), as we saw. This is why Rome, or, more precisely, Roma, is a 'whore' in Revelation – indeed, the 'great whore' (17.1; 19.2), the 'mother of whores' (17.5). Rome is the embodiment, for John, of repellent seductiveness. Beyond that, the spectacle of a highly sexualized female utterly out of (male) control serves, for John, as a convenient metaphor for Roman power. Under emperors such as Nero (to name only the emperor who casts the longest shadow over Revelation), Roman imperial power was absolute power exercised to excess, employed without restraint.

John expects that Rome, represented as a hyper-promiscuous woman (14.8; 17.1-2, 4; 18.3, 9; 19.2), will arouse in his audience the same loathing and disgust that he feels for her and it. Having constructed Rome as a female sex monster, a seething morass of unregulated sexual passions, John devises what he deems to be a suitable fate for her. 'Render to her as she herself has rendered', a 'voice from heaven' proclaims, 'repay her double for her deeds; mix a double draught for her in the cup she mixed' (18.6), that cup being 'full of abominations and the impurities of her fornications' (17.4). John's implied (male) audience is foaming at the mouth by now for suitably sexualized vengeance, and it is not disappointed. The woman is violently stripped, sexually shamed and physically annihilated. Paradoxically, the agents of her obliteration are the woman's closest associates who are infected by the same savage loathing for her that John seeks to inculcate in his implied audience: 'And the ten horns that you saw, they and the beast will loathe [*misēsousin*] the whore, and they will ravage her and strip her naked [*kai ērēmōnenēn poiēsousin autēn kai gymnēn*], and they will devour her flesh and burn her with fire' (17.16, my trans.). It all amounts to a prime lesson from the handbook of male misogyny on how to deal with a 'whore'.

Many feminist critics of Revelation have read the Babylon-as-whore-soon-to-get-her-comeuppance imagery, and other such material in the book, as firmly situated in the sordid biblical tradition long ago dubbed 'pornoprophetics' (see Selvidge 1996; Vander Stichele 2009: 109–14) and exemplified by similarly scarlet passages in Jeremiah, Ezekiel, Hosea and Nahum. Catherine Keller, in particular, has declined to put too fine a point on Rev. 17.16: "In God's name, a powerful, sexual, bejeweled woman is stripped, humiliated, and devoured by hairy and horny beasts. Vision becomes voyeurism: a pious snuff picture unfolds' (1996: 76). Other feminist critics have argued that Revelation is a thoroughly inhospitable and highly dangerous space for women (e.g., Pippin 1992, 1999: 78–127; Ipsen 2009: 166–204). Anything symbolized as female in Revelation is an object of violent loathing – also recall 'Jezebel … throw[n] on a bed' while her children are struck dead (2.20-3a) and the 144,000 male virgins 'who have not defiled themselves with women' (14.4a) – except when it assumes the patriarchally approved forms of virgin bride (19.7-8; 21.2, 9) or self-sacrificing mother (12.1-6, 13-17). Still other feminist critics have disagreed, arguing that the violence in Rev. 17.16, for example, is directed at a city, not a woman (see esp. Rossing 1999a: 87–97 passim), and generally resisting the attribution to Revelation of a pernicious gender ideology (see esp. Schüssler Fiorenza 2007: 130–47 passim). At issue ultimately in the debate is whether or to what extent gendered literary metaphors have real-world repercussions for contemporary women and men.

Not all who have engaged critically with the figure of Babylon, however, have been neatly lined up on one side or the other of the exegetical divide: Babylon as compelling counter-imperial image versus Babylon as misogynistic fantasy object. Babylon is a fleshed-out female character, by ancient standards, as well as a larger than life character, and as such overflows tidy antithetical conceptual boxes. Rather remarkably, indeed, this symbolic woman receives almost as much narrative space in the New Testament as Mary the mother of Jesus (whose main vehicle is the Lukan infancy narrative) and considerably more than Mary Magdalene (whose main scene is Jn 20.1-2, 11-18).

No one has exploited Babylon's relative complexity more thoroughly than womanist New Testament scholar Shanell T. Smith, for whom Babylon is at once an empress and a brothel slave and as such simultaneously situated 'on both sides of the colonial relationship', representing 'both the colonizer and the colonized' (2014: 127). Babylon is explicitly styled an empress in Rev. 18.7 ('I rule as a *basilissa* [empress/queen]') and implicitly styled a brothel slave in 17.5 ('and on her forehead was written a name, a mystery: "Babylon the great, mother of whores and of earth's abominations"'). Smith is following Jennifer Glancy and Stephen Moore, who in turn are following classicist C. P. Jones (1987: 151), in reading that forehead inscription as a slave tattoo, such facial tattooing being part and parcel of the brutal realities of slave prostitution in the Roman world, and almost all prostitutes in that world being slaves. Throughout antiquity, indeed, *pornē*, the term John uses for the woman Babylon (17.1, 5, 15-16; 19.2), was so commonly associated with slavery that it should be understood as denoting a brothel slave rather than a courtesan, contrary to what most scholars have traditionally supposed (see further Glancy and Moore 2011).

Smith goes farther than Glancy and Moore, however, by adding an autobiographical layer to this line of interpretation. Indeed, 'it's more than just interpretive business', for Smith; 'it's personal' (2014: 175). As a female African American descendent of slaves, Smith finds herself identifying profoundly with the slave woman Babylon. Smith writes: 'Denoting a female slave, violently abused and regarded as utterly dispensable, I ... know her story, and I empathize with her plight' (2014: 129). But Smith's felt identification with the woman Babylon is considerably more complex than that. Describing herself as 'a privileged black woman' (2014: 167), a socioeconomic beneficiary of the American Empire, Smith also feels 'loosely bound', at least, to the woman Babylon's other aspect as emblem of empire (2014: 167). Smith confesses: 'The economic *excess*ibility of the woman Babylon [see Rev. 18.11-13] highlights my association with empire, and I am distressed about it' (2014: 170). Smith concludes her extended reflection on this conflict, one that compels her to bring the categories of race, ethnicity and class to bear on Rev. 17–18 in addition to the more usual category of empire, as follows:

And I am filled with emotions from dejection and rage about all that I as a black woman have had to deal with, to contentment and gratitude regarding the benefits and privileges I receive from the capitalist system of America, to disbelief and confusion that I have so much in common with such a negatively regarded figure – the woman Babylon. I have come face to face in what [Clarice] Martin calls 'an unclouded mirror' [Martin 2005], seeing an almost the same, but not quite, reflection of myself. And I love her. (2014: 174)

The book of blood

The woman Babylon escapes John's iron grip in Shanell Smith's imaginative appropriation of her. Other elements of John's anti-imperial rhetoric also elude his control and, when pressed, collapse under the weight of their own internal contradictions. In particular, consider John's impassioned desire to see the Roman Empire substituted with a Messianic Empire. This desire is articulated explicitly in Rev. 11.15: 'The world empire [*hē basileia tou kosmou*] has become the empire of our Lord and his Messiah' (see also 1.5a; 12.10; 17.14; 19.16; 21.24). The two empires, however, are not easily disentangled.

To begin with, 'Lord' (Hebrew: *adon[ai]* and Greek: *kyrios*) is a recurrent appellative for the deity in the Jewish scriptures, and (in its Latin form, *dominus*) was also an honorific title embraced by certain Roman emperors, Nero in particular. It was rejected by other emperors, however, because it was seen in the political realm as a synonym for 'tyrant' (*tyrannus*; see esp. Pliny, *Panegyric* 2.3), while in the nonpolitical realm it connoted a master of slaves (which is what Revelation's God also is, as it happens: 1.1; 6.11; 7.3; 10.7; 11.18; 15.3; 19.2, 5, 10; 22.3, 6, 9; see also 2.20). But the Roman qualities of Revelation's deity, 'the one seated on the throne', go far beyond his *kyrios* title. As commentators have long noted, Revelation's heavenly liturgy, centred on this enthroned figure, is modelled in part on the ceremonial language and rituals of the Roman imperial court. For example, the acclamation, 'You are worthy', addressed to God or the Lamb by the heavenly courtiers assembled around the divine throne (4.11; 5.9; see also 5.12), was also used formally in the Roman court to greet the emperor. The title 'our Lord and God' (4.11; cf. Jn 20.28) was also applied to the Emperor Domitian (under whose reign Revelation may have achieved its final form) by members of his court (see esp. Martial, *Epigrams* 5.8; 7.34; 8.2; 9.66; 10.72). The twenty-four elders' gesture of casting their crowns or wreaths (*stephanoi*) before the throne, meanwhile (Rev. 4.10), corresponds with a form of obeisance offered to Roman emperors.

Such parallels prompt one to ask whether or to what extent Revelation's conception of the divine empire – 'the empire of our Lord and his Messiah' (11.15) – is anything more than human empire magnified, and consequently whether Revelation's theological vision can be classified as authentically counter-imperial. John's intention, presumably, in partially modelling God's heavenly court on the Roman imperial court was to represent the former as possessed of a glory that immeasurably exceeds the latter. By turning the Roman court into a blueprint for the heavenly court, however, John constructs a representation of the divine that is human, all too human – and not only because the divine emperor demands the same slavish treatment from his subordinates as the Roman emperor does. The larger problem is that God's Empire, as John constructs it, not only exceeds the Roman Empire in *glory* by orders of magnitude but it also exceeds the Roman Empire in *violence* by the same measure. John paradoxically projects the capacity for deadly, destructive violence, arguably the most unholy and ungodly human trait, onto the deity on a spectacular scale.

For John, Babylon is a cautionary symbol of Rome's seductiveness, as we saw. But John himself is not immune to Rome's seductions, as we are beginning to see. It is not her civic culture that seduces him, however, but rather her military might. Essentially, Revelation's Messianic Empire will be established by the same means through which the Roman Empire was established: war and conquest, entailing mass-slaughter, but now on a hyperbolic scale. Indeed, Revelation may be judged the most violent book in the entire Bible, the consummate book of blood, if violence is to be measured by such criteria as implicit mountains of human corpses (e.g., 6.3-4, 7-8; 9.13-19; 14.20; 19.11-21; 20.7-9) and mass extinction of nonhuman species (e.g., 8.7-12; 16.3-4, 8-9), culminating in the climactic obliteration of the entire earth (21.1). The relentless, rising wave of violence that propels the plot of Revelation forward from the breaking of the first seal (6.1-2) onwards emanates mainly from the reclusive divine being obliquely referred to as 'the one seated on the throne' and his improbable military commander, the Lamb. Their principal activities throughout Revelation are essentially imperial activities: the conduct of war and the enlargement of empire. More than any other early Christian text, indeed, Revelation is replete with the language of war and conquest. In this respect, it is, paradoxically, the most Roman of Roman books.

The Lamb has been waging its campaign since its first appearance in the heavenly throne room (5.6-14). Its innocuous-seeming activity of unsealing the seven seals that bound the eschatological scroll with which it had been entrusted has resulted in successive acts of destruction on a cosmic scale, including (but not limited to) 'peace [being taken] from the earth, so that people would slaughter one another' (6.4; see also 6.8); the sun becoming 'black as sackcloth', the moon 'like blood', the stars falling to earth, the sky vanishing 'like a scroll rolling itself up', and every mountain and island being 'removed from its place' (6.12-14); the issuing of seven trumpets to seven angels, the successive blowing of which triggers a further, yet more shocking sequence of cataclysmic disasters (8.1–9.20); and so on. As we progress from the seven seals to the seven trumpets and on to the seven bowls of God's wrath poured out upon the earth (15.5–16.21), the Lamb largely recedes from view. But the narrative leaves its audience in no doubt that the successive strikes against the earth and its inhabitants all issue ultimately from the military command post that the heavenly throne room has become and whose joint chiefs are 'the one seated on the throne' and the Lamb.

In 14.9-11, the Lamb's actions against its enemies take an especially disturbing form, as we saw earlier. They are sentenced to eternal torture 'with fire and sulfur in the presence of the holy angels and in the presence of the Lamb, … the smoke of their torture [*basanismos*] [going] up forever and ever' (14.10-11; cf. *1 Enoch* 54.1-2; 100.9; *4 Ezra* 7.36-8; *2 Baruch* 59.2). The combination of fire and sulfur seems to derive from the divine destruction of the cities of Sodom and Gomorrah and their inhabitants (see Gen. 19.24). Now, however, the punitive fire is unleashed more directly on the bodies of the damned, and those bodies, although burning, will never be consumed, the Lamb itself presiding over this unending atrocity.

Revelation's next verse, 14.12, which brings the episode to a close, reads: 'Here is a call for the endurance [*hypomonē*] of the saints, those who keep the commandments of God and hold fast to the faith of Jesus.' Why should the promise of eternal torment for the followers of the beast inspire endurance in the followers of the Lamb (see also 13.10, together with 1.9; 2.2-3, 19; 3.10)? Presumably, because it is an implicit answer to the plea for justice and vengeance earlier made by 'those who had been slaughtered for the word of God and for the testimony they had given' (6.9-10). Later Christian authorities, beginning with Tertullian and including Augustine and Aquinas, who declared that the bliss of the saints in heaven partially consists in beholding the torments of the damned in hell, perfectly captured the spirit of Revelation in this regard. Tertullian, imagining himself already enjoying the spectacle, expresses his joy on seeing 'so many illustrious monarchs … groaning now in the lowest darkness … ; governors of [Roman] provinces, too, who persecuted the Christian name, in fires more fierce than those …

they caused to rage against the followers of Christ' – and so on down the list of enemies, Tertullian exultantly 'fix[ing] a gaze insatiable' on their fiery sufferings (*The Shows* 30.3, 5; ANF trans., lightly modified).

With Rev. 14.9-12, however, the proleptic scene of punitive mass-torture we have been considering, we have vaulted forward in time to the Last Judgment, which is fully unveiled only in 20.11-15 and which entails 'anyone whose name [is] not found written in the book of life [being] thrown into the lake of fire'. This is a particularly arresting example of Revelation's long-remarked spiral structure, its eschewal of a strictly sequential or linear plot in favour of one studded with anticipatory and retrospective scenes.

The spiral structure continues after the mass-torture spectacle of 14.9-12. Following a further angelic announcement (14.13), we are returned to a scene that precedes the Last Judgment and its fiery punishments by more than a thousand years. Revelation 14.14-16 is, indeed, the first depiction in the book of Jesus' return in glory, a preview of 19.11-21, the latter being the full narrative unfolding of that epochal return, which itself precedes the millennium (20.4-6). Revelation 14.14-16 is also the only scene between Revelation 5 and Revelation 19 in which Jesus is not in his lamb form. He temporarily abandons his lamb guise here and reappears as 'one like a Son of Man', recapitulating 1.13, his initial appearance to John, in which that title was also used. He is even more Son-of-Man-like in 14.14, indeed, because like Daniel's Son of Man, he now comes on a cloud (see Dan. 7.13; cf. Rev. 1.7). The sharp sickle he holds, however, is borrowed from Joel 3.13.

The ensuing scene (Rev. 14.17-20) takes one of the more violent images in the Hebrew Bible – Yahweh as divine warrior trampling his enemies in the winepress of his wrath, their 'juice spatter[ing his] garments' and 'stain[ing his] robes', for 'vengeance [is] in [his] heart', causing him to '[crush] them … and [pour] out their lifeblood' (Isa. 63.1-6; cf. Lam. 1.15; Joel 3.13) – and exponentially amplifies its already considerable horror quotient. Revelation's Son of Man, aided by an angel also equipped with a sharp sickle, reaps the earth's (human) harvest and casts it into 'the great wine press of the wrath of God' (14.16, 19). And blood deluges from the winepress 'as high as a horse's bridle, for a distance of one thousand six hundred stadia [about 200 miles]" (14.20; cf. *1 Enoch* 100.1-3; *4 Ezra* 15.35-6). The scene previews Rev. 19.11-16, Jesus' eschatological advent at the head of 'the armies of heaven' to do battle with the beast and its armies. The reference to 'a horse's bridle' in 14.20 anticipates the detail of Jesus and the armies of heaven all being mounted on white steeds (19.11, 14) (as first noted in Charles 1920, II, 26), while it is said of the eschatological warrior that 'he will tread the wine press of the fury of the wrath of God the Almighty' (19.15). The deluge of blood in 14.20, then, flows from Revelation's Battle of battles in which God's preeminent agent will annihilate God's enemies. The colossal cascade of human blood 'as high as a horse's bridle' (14.20) merges with the sea that has become blood – 'like the blood of a corpse', indeed (16.3; see also 8.9); with 'the rivers and the springs of water' that have likewise become blood (16.4; see also 11.6); and with every other body of blood in this blood-sodden book.

In 6.15-16, right after the martyrs under the heavenly altar have cried out for divine justice and vengeance (6.9-11), the kings of the earth and all their minions call to the mountains: 'Fall on us and hide us from the face of the one seated on the throne and from the wrath of the Lamb; for the great day of their wrath has come, and who is able to stand?' In 19.11-21, the great day of wrath is fully revealed, and for the occasion, appropriately enough, the Lamb shrugs off its woolly costume and reappears in humanoid form. For the Lamb is not so much a wolf in sheep's clothing as a human animal in sheep's clothing. As slaughtered sheep, Revelation's protagonist embodies the human animal at its most vulnerable, its perpetual capacity to become a victim, to abruptly lose its life. As slaughtering warrior, however, Revelation's protagonist embodies the human animal's unparalleled savagery and capacity for vengeance. This warrior 'is clothed in a robe dipped in blood' (19.13). Whether the blood is his own or that of his enemies is a moot distinction. Even if it is his own blood, it will soon be mixed with enemy blood.

The implicit, but wholly palpable, theme of vengeance in Revelation's climactic representation of Jesus' Second Coming or parousia – a theme that has been gathering force throughout the entire narrative – requires both that Revelation's parousia take the form of a mighty, annihilating battle with its attendant horrors ('all the birds that fly in midheaven' being invited to feast on the mountain of dead flesh that God's enemies are about to become – 19.17-18) and that Jesus himself take the form of a celestial superwarrior. The theme of vengeance – one indissolubly bound up with blood in Revelation ('How long will it be before you judge and avenge our blood?' – 6.10; 'Because they shed ... blood ..., you have given them blood to drink. It is what they deserve!' – 16.6; 'He has avenged on [the great whore] the blood of his slaves' – 19.2) – is also what distinguishes Revelation's parousia from the Pauline and Synoptic parousias (see esp. 1 Thess. 4.16-17; Mt. 24.30-1; 25.31-3; Mk 13.26-7; Lk. 17.24; 21.27). The Pauline or Synoptic Christs are content to gather the elect on their return, or, at most, to preside as judge. Before the Last Judgment, however, Revelation's Christ first needs to wreak frightful vengeance on his foes.

The ecoapocalypse of John

Eschatology and ecology are intimately intertwined in Revelation. What tale does Revelation tell about the earth? What agency does Revelation ascribe to the earth? The latter question is prompted by two of the six 'ecojustice principles' formulated by the Earth Bible Team, a group of biblical ecotheologians and ecocritics whose work was catalytic for the first wave of ecological hermeneutics. According to 'the Principle of Voice', the earth 'is a subject capable of raising its voice in celebration and against injustice'; and according to 'the Principle of Resistance', the earth 'not only suffer[s] from injustices at the hands of humans, but actively resist[s] them in the struggle for justice' (Earth Bible Team 2000: 46, 52).

Several New Testament texts attribute such agency to the earth. The earth shakes and quakes at Jesus' crucifixion and resurrection (Mt. 27.51, 54; 28.2), and the sea will roar at his Second Coming while the heavenly bodies shudder (Lk. 21.25-6). The earth also erupts to unsettle the foundations of the prison in which Paul and Silas are being unjustly held (Acts 16.25-6). And in Rom. 8.18-23, the earth, here named the creation (*hē ktisis*; cf. Rev. 3.14), 'waits with eager longing for the revealing of the children of God', but also for its own liberation from 'its bondage to decay' (Rom. 8.19, 21; cf. Gen. 3.17-18). The creation 'groan[s] in labor pains', indeed, as it awaits this rebirth (Rom. 8.22).

In Revelation, meanwhile, the earth comes to the aid of one who has just endured labour and given birth and whose infant is threatened with death: 'But the earth [*hē gē*] came to the help of the woman [who, among her many identities, is Mary the mother of Jesus, as we have seen]; it opened its mouth and swallowed the river that the dragon [Satan] had poured from its mouth' (12.16). Here the earth is more fully personified than in any other New Testament text. In ancient Greek mythology the earth was Gaia, a high goddess, one of the primordial deities who had existed since the dawn of creation. Earth is also a woman in Rev. 12.16, where she empathetically and spectacularly comes to the rescue of another woman who, as we also saw, happens herself to be a goddess. Although fleeting, the moment is significant. Steven J. Friesen (2001: 186), indeed, has styled earth a fifth (and thoroughly neglected) major female figure in Revelation, together with Jezebel, the Woman Clothed with the Sun, Babylon and the Bride.

Let us trace the journey of this neglected female character, earth, through the plot of Revelation. As we shall see, she turns out to be an extraordinarily tenacious figure. The odds against her survival are considerable at every turn. To that extent, she is an apt stand-in for the contemporary earth, the beleaguered planet that birthed us all, whose future is currently so uncertain.

To begin with the basics, Revelation sets off unnerving alarm bells for many contemporary Christians who care about the survival of our planet. Repeatedly, Revelation's prophetic visions are of the destruction of the earth – indeed, of the entire cosmos. Let us review some of the main assaults. The opening of the sixth seal (6.12-17) precipitates the first sequence of Revelation's many cosmic disasters. The sun, moon, stars and sky all undergo destruction in ways standard for the eschatological 'day of the Lord' as described in the Hebrew Scriptures (e.g., Joel 2.10-11, 30-1; Isa. 13.9-10; 34.4; Ezek. 32.7-8). Immediately thereafter, four angels are 'given power to damage earth and sea' (Rev. 7.2). Although earth and sea are granted a reprieve (7.3), it is only temporary.

Revelation's most spectacular ecocidal visions are concentrated in the seven trumpets and seven bowls sequences. Both the trumpet eco-catastrophes and the bowl eco-catastrophes are hyperbolic reenactments of the 'plagues' (the standard English translation of several Hebrew terms) inflicted on Egypt by God and Moses in the exodus narrative (Exod. 7.1–15.21). Indeed, the trumpet and bowl cataclysms are also styled 'plagues' (*plēgai*, which, however, can also mean 'blows', 'wounds' or 'afflictions') in Revelation (9.18, 20; 15.1, 6, 8; 16.9, 21).

The first trumpet-induced disaster (Rev. 8.7) is modelled on the plague of hail in the exodus saga (Exod. 9.22-5). The blowing of the first trumpet causes a third of the earth, including a third of the trees and 'all green grass', to be 'burned up' (Rev. 8.7). The second trumpet cataclysm (8.8-9) is modelled on the plague of blood (Exod. 7.20-1). It causes a third of the sea to become blood and a third of its creatures to perish (Rev. 8.9; see also 11.6). The third trumpet cataclysm – a 'great star' falls from heaven, poisoning a third of the earth's rivers (Rev. 8.10-11) – has no precise Exodus parallel (but see Jer. 9.15; 23.15). The fourth trumpet cataclysm (Rev. 8.12) is modelled on the plague of darkness (Exod. 10.21-3), while the fifth (Rev. 9.1-11) is a particularly arresting example of how John transforms Exodus's localized plagues into cosmic and eschatological events. Exodus's destructive but mundane locusts (Exod. 10.4-6, 12-15; see also Joel 1.4) morph into demonic monsters in Revelation, supernatural in origin and terrifying in appearance. Revelation's sixth trumpet cataclysm (Rev. 9.13-17) extends the orgiastic violence of the fifth and is likewise levelled directly at human beings 'who do not have the seal of God on their foreheads', while the demon cavalry is also ordered 'not to damage the grass of the earth or any green growth or any tree' (9.4; see also 7.3) – a little late, however, since 'all green grass' has already been 'burned up' in the first trumpet catastrophe, along with 'a third of the earth' and 'a third of the trees' (8.7).

Remarkably, it all happens all over again in Revelation 16, the seven angels relentlessly pouring out their seven bowls overflowing with 'God's wrath' on the already horribly damaged earth and finishing what the seven trumpet-angels had begun. Most notably, whereas the blowing of the second trumpet had caused 'a third of the sea [to become] blood' and 'a third of the living creatures in the sea [to die]' (8.9), the pouring out of the second bowl now causes the entire sea to become 'like the blood of a corpse' and all sea life to perish (16.3), while the third bowl causes all the rivers and springs to become blood (16.4). In an eerie anticipation of global warming, the fourth bowl even causes the climate to become dangerously overheated (16.8-9).

This all leads inexorably to what appears at first glance to be an obituary for 'the first earth': 'Then I saw a new heaven and a new earth [*ouranon kainon kai gēn kainēn*]; for the first heaven and the first earth had passed away, and the sea was no more' (21.1; cf. Isa. 65.17; 66.22). 'We have only one planet', contemporary eco-activists insist. Not in Revelation, it would seem, a particularly dangerous facet of the earth tale it seems to tell. Does Revelation, with a wave of its narrative wand, magically replace the earth it has systematically rendered uninhabitable? In the book's climactic vision, are 'the first heaven and the first earth' simply removed, demolished and hauled away, and the sea somehow siphoned off, to clear a site for 'the new heaven and new earth' in a cosmic real estate teardown?

This, however, is not the only possible reading of the plot and denouement of Revelation's epic tale of earth. As with any other biblical text, alternative interpretations are always possible and often necessary. Barbara R. Rossing, in particular, has argued that Revelation is not anti-earth but merely anti-imperial (see also Kiel 2017: 57-88). Rossing assigns pivotal significance to the statement that follows the blowing of the seventh trumpet: '[God's] wrath has come, and the time ... for destroying those who destroy the earth [*tēn gēn*]' (Rev. 11.18). Who are these destroyers of the earth? Rossing's answer (2002, 2005) is the Romans. They depleted and poisoned the natural environment throughout the Mediterranean basin through such practices as clear-cutting forests, over-mining metals, polluting water sources and decimating animal populations. These destructive practices are implied in the 'cargo list' of Rev. 18.11-13, which lists the profusion of luxury goods demanded by elite Romans to maintain their privileged lifestyle. According to Rossing, then, the calamities precipitated by the trumpets and bowls are not directed at the earth but rather at the Romans who exploit the earth. Like the plagues of Exodus, moreover, the plagues of Revelation are designed to elicit repentance (Rev. 9.20-1; 16.8-11; cf. Exod. 7.13-14, 22; 8:15, etc.).

Rossing never fully comes to grips, however, with the problem of collateral damage, which, like so much else in Revelation, is cosmically colossal: in destroying the destroyers of the earth, God's angelic agents systematically make the earth uninhabitable even for the victims of those destroyers, both human and nonhuman victims alike, and eventually themselves destroy the earth outright with a terrifying thoroughness of which the human destroyers would not have been capable. It is not only the human enemies of God and the Lamb who bleed in Revelation, then, their 'blood flow[ing] … as high as a horse's bridle, for a distance of about two hundred miles' (14.20). The earth bleeds even more profusely in Revelation. It bleeds oceans of blood, rivers of blood (8.9; 16.3-4). And it burns (8.5-8; 16.8-9) even while drowning in its own blood.

Yet, somehow, the earth manages to rise from its own ashes – from *her* own ashes – in Revelation, proving spectacularly tenacious, clinging stubbornly to life against overwhelming death-dealing odds. The Lamb that stands, that lives, even though slaughtered is held up in Rev. 5 as an object for cosmic wonder. But the earth endures far more in Revelation, being slaughtered many times over. The first evidence of the earth's dogged refusal to die comes in Rev. 20, a chapter that, at first blush, might not seem to have much to do with matters ecological. The most prominent elements of the chapter are its presentation of the millennium (20.4-6), followed by the Last Judgment (20.11-15). The millennium is, as we have seen, the traditional name for Jesus' thousand-year co-reign with the resurrected martyrs (20.4-5) once Satan has been imprisoned in 'the bottomless pit' (20.1-3). Where, precisely, will Jesus and his faithful followers reign? Revelation doesn't say explicitly, but reign on earth – as opposed, say, to in heaven – is the implicit answer. It fits both the immediate context – after the thousand years, Satan will be released and will begin once more to 'deceive the nations of … the earth' that had been spared his attentions during the millennium (20.7-8; see also 20.3) – and the larger context: Revelation nowhere situates the redeemed in a heavenly afterlife, as we shall see. None of this should surprise us. The notion of a visible reign of God on earth – a 'heaven on earth' – is one with deep roots in the prophetic literature of the Hebrew Bible (see esp. Isa. 11.6-9; 65.17-25; Ezek. 34.25-31), and is also picked up in other apocalyptic literature contemporary with Revelation: *2 Baruch* describes an eschatological, but earthly, messianic kingdom that will endure for an unspecified, but temporary, period of time (29.3–30.1), while *4 Ezra* describes an earthly messianic kingdom that will last 400 years (7.26-30).

The relevance of all of this for ecotheology and ecocriticism is that earth is not about to vanish in Revelation's climactic scenes. She is not about to slip unobtrusively off the stage or explode in a ball of fire (as in 2 Pet. 3.7, 10, 12) just because Jesus has returned in glory (Rev. 19.11ff.). The earth will endure and her human inhabitants will have changed, human warfare no longer being waged (as 20.7-8 implies). *2 Baruch* extends the transformation motif beyond the human realm, representing the blessings of the interim messianic kingdom in terms of a superabundant earth: 'The earth … shall yield its fruit ten-thousandfold, and on each vine there shall be a thousand branches, and each branch shall produce a thousand clusters, and each cluster shall produce a thousand grapes, and each grape shall produce a cor [around 60 gallons] of wine' (29.5; trans. from Charles 1913, II). In *2 Baruch's* exuberant apocalyptic imagination, the earth, far from disintegrating or burning up at the consummation of history, becomes an almost excessively productive super-earth, a true Gaia goddess, reducing its human inhabitants to the status of awed admirers of her wonders: 'They shall behold marvels every day!' (29.6). Revelation holds its own description of a transformed earth over for 21.1–22.5, as we shall see, its depiction of the eternal messianic kingdom for which the millennial kingdom is only a prelude. Still, in Revelation's depiction of the millennium there is, implicitly, still an earth, and in light of all the ecocidal assaults that have preceded the millennium, that is not the least of this book's marvels.

The earth plays a still more occluded, but also significant, role in the Last Judgment panorama (20.11-15) that follows the millennium. Earth is not mentioned in that scene, but Hades is mentioned twice in it (20.13-14; see also 1.18; 6.8; Mt. 11.23; 16.18; Lk. 10.15; 16.23; Acts 2.27, 31). Hades should not be confused with the Christian concept of hell. Hell corresponds to Revelation's 'lake of fire' (20.15; see also 19.20; 20.10; 21.8). At the Last Judgment, Hades, together with Death, is thrown into the lake of fire (20.14). Hades was the ancient Greek term for the underworld, the general abode of the dead, good and bad alike. As such, Hades is also the term ordinarily used to translate the Hebrew word Sheol in the Septuagint, the ancient Greek translation of the Hebrew Scriptures, since Sheol was also conceived as a dark, subterranean realm to which all the dead went, wicked and virtuous alike (e.g., Num. 16.23-33; Ps. 88.1-12; Eccl. 9.1-10; Isa. 38.10-11, 18-19). After the general resurrection of the dead and the Last Judgment

(Rev. 20.12-13), people will no longer die, so Hades, the holding place of the dead, will no longer be needed, which is why Revelation disposes of it (20.14; cf. *4 Ezra* 8:53), casts it into the divine incinerator.

If those who have escaped the lake of fire (see Rev. 20.15) are not to live out eternity, then, in a great gloomy underground cavern, where are they destined to live it out? Not in heaven either, in the sense of an otherworldly place above the sky, or in the sense of a purely 'spiritual' place different and separate from any earthly space. Rather, Revelation's redeemed are destined to live out eternity upon a transformed earth. The earth is not dispensable, ultimately, even in this most apocalyptic of biblical books. Admittedly, the earth featured in Rev. 21–22 is not the same earth featured in Revelation 1–20: 'Then I saw a new heaven and a new earth; for the first heaven and the first earth had passed away' (21.1). But the substitution, the teardown, proves to be unnecessary. What now transpires on this 'new' earth might just as easily have been staged on the 'old' earth. 'There is no Planet B', climate activists proclaim. Revelation's Planet B, its 'new earth', is a superfluous concept, as we are about to see.

Revelation 21.1–22.5 describes the second, postmillennial, permanent phase of the establishment of heaven on earth. In Revelation's final vision, the 'redeemed' followers of the Lamb (14.3-4) are not whisked up to heaven, as John himself was in 4.1-2. There is no Rapture in Revelation, as Rossing has rightly insisted (2007), the Rapture scenario stemming instead, as we saw earlier, from 1 Thess. 4.15-17. Rather, in Revelation, heaven descends to (a recreated) earth in the form of the New Jerusalem (21.1-2; see also 3.12). This 'holy city' (21.2, 10, 19) is the new dwelling place of God and the Lamb (21.22-3; 22.3-5). And also of the redeemed? Not quite. The redeemed do not dwell *in* the New Jerusalem with God and the Lamb; rather, the redeemed *are* the New Jerusalem, and God and the Lamb dwell in them.

The New Jerusalem, as the redeemed people of God, is represented as the bride of Christ – 'I saw ... the New Jerusalem ... prepared as a bride adorned for her husband' (21.2; see also 19.7; 21.9) – just as in other early Christian literature (e.g., 2 Cor. 11.2; Eph. 5.25-7). Other details of the city's description also evoke the people of God. On its twelve gates are inscribed the names of the twelve tribes of Israel (Rev. 21.12), while on the twelve foundations of its wall are inscribed 'the ... names of the 12 apostles of the Lamb' (21.14; cf. Eph. 2.19-20). The twelve jewels that adorn the foundations correspond to the twelve jewels on the breastplate of Israel's high priest (Rev. 21.19-20; cf. Exod. 28.15-21; 39.8-14). This in turn evokes Revelation's description of the redeemed as a company of priests (Rev. 1.6; 5.10; 20.6; cf. 1 Pet. 2.5, 9). In short, Revelation's New Jerusalem is an elaborate, multifaceted symbol for the eschatological people of God (see further Gundry 2005). Revelation 21 thus decoded announces that, following the Last Judgment (which takes place in a mysterious no place, neither earth nor heaven – 20.11), those whose names have been 'found written in the book of life' (20.15) will be beamed down to a recreated earth, a customized Planet B, to live out immortal lives on its surface, 'death [now] be[ing] no more' (21.4). What will be the conditions of this eternal existence?

The most enticing scene in Revelation for those attempting, whether in sermon or in scholarship, to use the book as a positive resource for ecotheology is Rev. 22.1-2, in which John is shown 'the river of the water of life' flowing through the heavenly city and 'the tree of life' with its healing leaves growing 'on either side of the river'. The immediate backdrop for the vision is Ezek. 47.1-12, an arresting image for ecological renewal of a fatally polluted planet, if ever there was one. The regenerative river of Ezekiel's vision will enter 'the sea of stagnant waters', causing the waters to 'become fresh', and 'wherever the river goes, every living creature that swarms will live' (47.8-9). Also flowing into Revelation's river of life is the primeval river that watered the Garden of Eden (Gen. 2.10). The tree of life formerly in Eden (Gen. 2.8-9; cf. 3.22-4) has also been transplanted to Revelation's heavenly city (Rev. 22.2, 14, 19; cf. *4 Ezra* 2.12; 8.51-2). The Christian Bible, as we like to say, ends as it began, in a garden. Revelation's Jesus describes the eternal abode of the blessed, indeed, as 'the *paradeisos* of God' (2.7) – God's paradise or, more literally, God's garden. The end time, according to Revelation, will entail a return of the primal time of creation.

Yet all is not so Edenic in Revelation's 'paradise of God'. Unlike the Garden of Eden, the garden of Rev. 22.1-2 is situated in a city, and the dimensions of this city are immense. In length, breadth and even height, the city is 12,000 stadia (21.15-16), a measurement approximately equal to 1,500 miles. Onto the surface of Planet B, then, a science fiction cube of surreally outsized proportions descends. Or to put it in more pedestrian terms, the river and tree of Revelation's climactic vision are located in a city whose length and breadth alone would encompass more than half of the continental United States, which begs the question: Is this a heavenly city or a hellish city? Is the vision of its descent to earth properly regarded as a hope-inspiring, action-impelling promise of release from our current ecocidal megacrisis? Or is this vision better construed instead as a cartoon rendering of rampant urbanization and its catastrophic consequences: a megalopolis beyond measure thudding down upon the natural world? The earth shudders and groans under its crushing weight. We would do well to listen to her cries.

Yes, this city is symbolic, as we have seen, but the specifics of Revelation's symbols matter. Otherwise, something like 'the Great Whore debate' that has raged in, and alongside, feminist scholarship on Revelation for the past thirty years would make no sense. Recognizing that the New Jerusalem is not an actual city does not dispose of the problem of its earth-obliterating size, any more than recognizing that Babylon is not an actual woman disposes of the problem of the misogynistic violence to which she is subjected. Metaphors matter. They embody and perpetuate ideologies and as such shape social, and even natural, worlds.

Yet, as we continue to stroll around the heavenly city we discover that it may not, after all, be an entirely bleak symbol for ecology. Yes, the city's excessive proportions do thoroughly overshadow the stream and tree it contains. Ecotheology shrivels in its shade and languishes in its suburbs. More promising for ecotheology than the heavenly city or the single stream or sole tree in the city park at its centre is the solitary animal in that park. This Central Park, it is important to note, does not contain a Central Park Zoo. This animal is not caged nor is it domesticated. It is not treated as an inferior being by humans, nor is it (any longer) in mortal danger from them. It does not grovel before humans; it does not flee from or cower in fear before them, nor is it dependent on them.

This doubly singular animal – sole and exceptional – is symbiotically conjoined with the divine (21.22-3; 22.1, 3). It is itself, indeed, divine. As such, it now determines the fate of humans, decides whether they live or die (21.27; cf. 13.8; 20.12, 15), in the same way that humans have perennially (and always too casually) determined the fate of (other) animals. Revelation, this book of divine vengeance, of just revenge, also ultimately stages the eschatological revenge of the animal (cf. 6.15-17). Human beings, enslavers of animals from the dawn of human history, now become slaves of the animal: 'But the throne of God and of the Lamb will be in [the city], and his slaves [*douloi*] will worship him' (22.3) – God and the Lamb here 'conceived so much as a unity that the singular pronoun can refer to both' (Beale 1999: 1,113; see also Slater 1999: 200). And just as humans have from ancient times branded domestic animals with marks of ownership, so will humans now bear a visible sign that they are the property, not only of God, but of a sheep: 'And his name will be on their foreheads' (22.4; see also 14.1).

All of this may sound like the script for a singularly schlocky eco-horror revenge movie. But the tale may also be told more positively. Jesus enters Revelation as 'one like a Son of Man' (1.12-13), transforms soon thereafter into a Lamb (5.6) and proceeds through the main body of the text in that four-legged form. He assumes human form again only in 14.14-16 and 19.11-21 (on both occasions, to mete out atrocious, death-dealing violence; what is it about human beings?). When the shape-shifting finally ends and Jesus is enthroned with God in the heavenly city as an object of eternal worship, he is in his animal form once more (22.1, 3). Intriguingly, it is only in animal guise that Jesus is worshipped anywhere in Revelation (5.8-14; 22.3). In other words, the principal christological image in Revelation is the image of a quadrupedal Christ, and this is the image of Jesus stamped most obviously with the mark of divinity in the book because it is the image explicitly marked for worship. Revelation's christology is high, as is customarily said; but it is highest of all when it is an animal christology. This needs to be said, and said often, in Christian circles in this age of mass extinction. It is the heavenly Lamb, not the city park in the heavenly megalopolis, that is the most apt ecological symbol provided by John's ecoapocalypse for our desperately damaged planet.

But what precisely might this entirely silent Lamb be telling us? We can never liberate it from its holding pen in the heavenly slaughterhouse. It was always too late for that; the lamb has always already been butchered long before we rise with John in the cloud elevator to behold it (4.1-2; 5.6-14). But that is precisely what makes the Lamb such a searingly effective symbol for the innumerable always-about-to-be-butchered-and/or-rendered-extinct nonhuman animals in our own (inhuman) world. Personally, I had long imagined that we might at least rescue Revelation's sheep from its violently vengeful fantasies. But now I'm not so sure. A cute, cuddly lamb now seems less relevant, ecotheologically speaking, than an angry lamb, a pissed-off sheep. The Lamb and all the nonhuman animal others for whom it stands – 'standing as though slain' (5.6) before that throne on which we ourselves are seated – have the power to hurt us, and hurt us horribly, but only because we are slaughtering or starving them to extinction and thereby dooming ourselves to having to live without them, which might not be a life worth living or any life at all. The more we continue to kill them off, then, the more we have reason to fear them. Revelation itself warns us to 'hide … from the wrath of the Lamb' (6.16). None of us should ever want to face an angry sheep – indeed, a ravening, rampaging, mass-killing sheep – perhaps the most alarming monster of all that this book of monsters has spawned.

Works Cited

Akenson, Donald Harman. 2018. *Exporting the Rapture: John Nelson Darby and the Victorian Conquest of North-American Evangelicalism* (Oxford, UK: Oxford University Press).

Aune, David E. 1997. *Revelation 1–5* (Word Biblical Commentary, 52A; Dallas: Word Books).

Aune, David E. 1998a. *Revelation 6–16* (Word Biblical Commentary, 52B; Nashville: Thomas Nelson).

Aune, David E. 1998b. *Revelation 17–22* (Word Biblical Commentary, 52C; Nashville: Thomas Nelson).

Bauckham, Richard. 1993. 'The Economic Critique of Rome in Revelation 18', in his *The Climax of Prophecy: Studies on the Book of Revelation* (New York: T&T Clark), 228–83.

Beal, Timothy. 2018. *The Book of Revelation: A Biography* (Princeton, NJ: Princeton University Press).

Beale, G. K. 1999. *The Book of Revelation: A Commentary on the Greek Text* (New International Greek New Testament Commentary; Grand Rapids, MI: Eerdmans).

Beale, G. K. 2010. *The Use of Daniel in Jewish Apocalyptic Literature and in the Revelation of St. John* (Eugene, OR: Wipf and Stock).

Beauvery, Robert. 1983. 'L'Apocalypse au risque de la numismatique: Babylone, la grand Prostituée et le sixiéme roi Vespasien et la déesse Rome', *Revue Biblique* 90: 243–60.

Blount, Brian K. 2001. *Then the Whisper Put on Flesh: New Testament Ethics in an African American Context* (Nashville: Abingdon Press, 2001).

Blount, Brian K. 2005a. *Can I Get a Witness? Revelation through African American Culture* (Louisville, KY: Westminster John Knox Press).

Blount, Brian K. 2005b. 'The Witness of Active Resistance: The Ethics of Revelation in African American Perspective', in *From Every People and Nation: The Book of Revelation in Intercultural Perspective* (ed. David Rhoads; Minneapolis: Fortress Press), 28–46.

Blount, Brian K. 2007. 'Revelation', in *True to Our Native Land: An African American New Testament Commentary* (ed. Brian K. Blount et al.; Minneapolis: Fortress Press), 523–57.

Blount, Brian K. 2009. *Revelation: A Commentary* (The New Testament Library; Louisville, KY: Westminster John Knox Press).

Boesak, Allan A. 1987. *Comfort and Protest: The Apocalypse from a South African Perspective* (Philadelphia: Westminster Press).

Boxall, Ian. 2013. *Patmos in the Reception History of the Apocalypse* (Oxford, UK: Oxford University Press).

Cady Stanton, Elizabeth et al. 1895–98. *The Woman's Bible* (2 vols.; New York: European Publishing Company).

Callahan, Allen Dwight. 1995. 'The Language of Apocalypse', *Harvard Theological Review* 88: 453–70.

Carrell, Peter R. 1997. *Jesus and the Angels: Angelology and the Christology of the Apocalypse of John* (Society for New Testament Studies Monograph Series, 95; Cambridge, UK: Cambridge University Press).

Carter, Warren. 2009. 'Accommodating "Jezebel" and Withdrawing John: Negotiating Empire in Revelation Then and Now', *Interpretation: A Journal of Bible and Theology* 63: 32–47.

Champlin, Edward. 2003. *Nero* (Cambridge, MA: Harvard University Press).

Charles, R. H., ed. 1913. *The Apocrypha and Pseudepigrapha of the Old Testament in English* (2 vols.; Oxford, UK: Oxford University Press).

Charles, R. H. 1920. *A Critical and Exegetical Commentary on the Revelation to St. John* (2 vols.; International Critical Commentary; Edinburgh: T&T Clark).

Charlesworth, James H., ed. 2010. *The Old Testament Pseudepigrapha*, Vol. 1: *Apocalyptic Literature and Testaments* (Peabody, MA: Hendrickson).

Clanton, Dan W., Jr., ed. 2012. *The End Will Be Graphic: Apocalyptic in Comic Books and Graphic Novels* (The Bible in the Modern World, 43; Sheffield, UK: Sheffield Phoenix).

Collins, John J., ed. 1979. *Apocalypse: The Morphology of a Genre* (Semeia, 14; Missoula, MT: Scholars Press).

Constantinou, Eugenia Scarvelis, trans. 2011. Andrew of Caesarea, *Commentary on the Apocalypse* (The Fathers of the Church: A New Translation, 123; Washington, DC: The Catholic University of America Press).

Darby, John Nelson. 1879–83. *The Collected Writings of John Nelson Darby* (ed. William Kelly; 47 vols.; Dublin: G. Morrish).

Darden, Lynne St. Clair. 2015. *Scripturalizing Revelation: An African American Postcolonial Reading of Empire* (Semeia Studies, 80; Atlanta: SBL Press).

Daynes, Sarah. 2010. *Time and Memory in Reggae Music: The Politics of Hope* (Manchester, UK: Manchester University Press).

Duff, Paul B. 2001. *Who Rides the Beast? Prophetic Rivalry and the Rhetoric of Crisis in the Churches of the Apocalypse* (Oxford, UK: Oxford University Press).

The Earth Bible Team. 2000. 'Guiding Ecojustice Principles', in *Readings from the Perspective of Earth* (ed. Norman C. Habel; Earth Bible, 1; Sheffield, UK: Sheffield Academic Press; Cleveland, OH: The Pilgrim Press), 38–53.

Eco, Umberto. 2003. 'Waiting for the Millennium', in *The Apocalyptic Year 1000: Religious Expectation and Social Change, 950–1050* (ed. Richard Landes, Andrew Gow, and David C. Van Meter; Oxford, UK: Oxford University Press), 121–37.

Emanuel, Sarah. 2020. *Humor, Resistance, and Jewish Cultural Persistence in the Book of Revelation: Roasting Rome* (Cambridge, UK: Cambridge University Press).

Evans, Tom. 2017. 'Is Trump REALLY the Antichrist? The Donald's Terrifying 666 Pattern Revealed', *Daily Star*, 19 January 2017: https://www.dailystar.co.uk/news/latest-news/563055/Donald-Trump-antichrist-satan-666-pattern-president-elect-Hillary-Clinton-occult-devil.

Feltoe, Charles Lett. 2015 [1918]. *St. Dionysius of Alexandria: Letters and Treatises* (Translations of Christian Literature, Series 1: Greek Texts; London: Aeterna Press).

Fletcher, Michelle. 2017. *Reading Revelation as Pastiche: Imitating the Past* (Library of New Testament Studies, 571; New York: T&T Clark).

Frankfurter, David. 2001. 'Jews or Not? Reconstructing the "Other" in Rev. 2:9 and 3:9', *Harvard Theological Review* 94: 403–25.

Frankfurter, David. 2011. 'The Revelation to John', in *The Jewish Annotated New Testament* (ed. Amy-Jill Levine and Marc Zvi Brettler; Oxford, UK: Oxford University Press), 463–98.

Friesen, Steven J. 2001. *Imperial Cults and the Apocalypse of John: Reading Revelation in the Ruins* (Oxford, UK: Oxford University Press).

Frykholm, Amy Johnson. 2004. *Rapture Culture: Left Behind in Evangelical America* (Oxford, UK: Oxford University Press).

Frykholm, Amy Johnson. 2014. 'Apocalypticism in Contemporary Christianity', in *The Oxford Handbook of Apocalyptic Literature* (ed. John J. Collins; Oxford, UK: Oxford University Press), 441–56.

Gilhus, Ingvild Saelid. 2006. *Animals, Gods and Humans: Changing Attitudes to Animals in Greek, Roman and Early Christian Ideas* (New York: Routledge).

Glancy, Jennifer A., and Stephen D. Moore. 2011. 'How Typical a Roman Prostitute Is Revelation's "Great Whore"?', *Journal of Biblical Literature* 130: 543–62.

Glynn, Kevin. 2000. *Tabloid Culture: Trash Taste, Popular Power, and the Transformation of American Television* (Durham, NC: Duke University Press).

Grant, Michael, trans. 1971. *Tacitus: The Annals of Imperial Rome* (rev. ed.; London: Penguin Books).

Graves, Robert, trans. 1957. *Suetonius: The Twelve Caesars* (West Drayton, UK: Penguin Books).

Gribben, Crawford. 2009. *Writing the Rapture: Prophecy Fiction in Evangelical America* (Oxford, UK: Oxford University Press).

Gundry, Robert H. 2005. 'The New Jerusalem: People as Place, Not Place for People', in his *The Old Is Better: New Testament Essays in Support of Traditional Interpretations* (Wissenshaftliche Untersuchungen zum Neuen Testament, 178; Tübingen: Mohr Siebeck), 399–412.

Hankins, Barry. 2008. 'Dispensational Premillennialism: Editorial Headnote', in *Evangelicalism and Fundamentalism: A Documentary Reader* (ed. Barry Hankins; New York: New York University Press), 59–60.

Hickson, Alex. 2017. 'Donald Trump Inauguration: John Titor "Time Traveller from 2036" about to Become President', *Daily Star*, 19 January 2017: https://www.dailystar.co.uk/news/latest-news/551048/John-Titor-Donald-Trump-time-traveller-mystery-warn-ISIS-nuclear-war-Nikola-Tesla-election.

Hidalgo, Jacqueline M. 2016. *Revelation in Aztlán: Scriptures, Utopias, and the Chicano Movement* (The Bible and Cultural Studies; New York: Palgrave Macmillan).

Howard, Robert Glenn, ed. 2011. *Network Apocalypse: Visions of the End in an Age of Internet Media* (The Bible in the Modern World, 36; Sheffield, UK: Sheffield Phoenix).

Howard-Brook, Wes, and Anthony Gwyther. 1999. *Unveiling Empire: Reading Revelation Then and Now* (Bible and Liberation; Maryknoll, NY: Orbis Books).

Huber, Lynn R. 2011. 'Gazing at the Whore: Reading Revelation Queerly', in *Bible Trouble: Queer Reading at the Boundaries of Biblical Scholarship* (ed. Teresa J. Hornsby and Ken Stone; Semeia Studies, 67; Atlanta: Society of Biblical Literature), 301–20.

Hungerford, Amy. 2010. *Postmodern Belief: American Literature and Religion since 1960* (Princeton, NJ: Princeton University Press).

Ipsen, Avaren. 2009. *Sex Working and the Bible* (BibleWorld; London: Equinox).

Johns, Loren L. 2003. *The Lamb Christology of the Apocalypse of John* (Wissenshaftliche Untersuchungen zum Neuen Testament, 167; Tübingen: Mohr Siebeck).

Jones, C. P. 1987. '*Stigma*: Tattooing and Branding in Graeco-Roman Antiquity', in *Aufstieg und Niedergang der römischen Welt: Geschichte und Kultur Roms im Spiegel der neueren Forschung* (ed. Hildegard Temporini and Wolfgang Haase; Berlin: De Gruyter), 23.2:1023–54.

Keller, Catherine. 1996. *Apocalypse Now and Then: A Feminist Guide to the End of the World* (Boston: Beacon Press).

Keller, Catherine. 2000. 'No More Sea: The Lost Chaos of the Eschaton', in *Christianity and Ecology: Seeking the Well-Being of Earth and Humans* (ed. Dieter T. Hessel and Rosemary Radford Ruether; Cambridge, MA: Harvard University Center for the Study of World Religions), 183–98.

Keller, Catherine. 2005. *God and Power: Counter-Apocalyptic Journeys* (Minneapolis: Fortress Press).

Kiel, Micah D. 2017. *Apocalyptic Ecology: The Book of Revelation, the Earth, and the Future* (Collegeville, MN: Liturgical Press).

Kim, Jean K. 1999. '"Uncovering Her Wickedness": An Inter(con)textual Reading of Revelation 17 from a Postcolonial Feminist Perspective', *Journal for the Study of the New Testament* 73: 61–81.

Koester, Craig R. 2014. *Revelation: A New Translation with Introduction and Commentary* (The Anchor Yale Bible; New Haven, CT: Yale University Press).

Kovacs, Judith, and Christopher Rowland. 2004. *Revelation* (Blackwell Bible Commentaries; Oxford, UK: Blackwell).

LaHaye, Tim, and Jerry B. Jenkins. 1995. *Left Behind: A Novel of the Earth's Last Days* (Wheaton, IL: Tyndale House).

Lester, Olivia Stewart. 2018. *Prophetic Rivalry, Gender, and Economics: A Study in Revelation and Sibylline Oracles 4–5* (Wissenschaftliche Untersuchungen zum Neuen Testament: 2 Reihe, 466; Tübingen: Mohr Siebeck).

Lindsey, Hal, with C. C. Carlson. 1970. *The Late Great Planet Earth* (Grand Rapids, MI: Zondervan).

Luther, Martin. 1960. 'Preface to the Revelation of St. John [2] 1546 (1530)', in *Luther's Works* (ed. E. T. Bachman; Philadelphia: Fortress Press), Vol. 35, *Word and Sacrament I*, 399–411.

Malkinson, Trevor. 2017. 'Come Out of Babylon: Heavy Metal Music and the Book of Revelation', *Metapsychosis: Journal of Consciousness, Literature, and Art*, 11 September 2017: https://www.metapsychosis.com/come-babylon-heavy-metal-music-book-revelation/.

Marshall, John W. 2001. *Parables of War: Reading John's Jewish Apocalypse* (Studies in Christianity and Judaism, 10; Waterloo, ON: Wilfred Laurier University Press).

Marshall, John W. 2007. 'John's Jewish (Christian?) Apocalypse', in *Jewish Christianity Reconsidered: Rethinking Ancient Groups and Texts* (ed. Matt A. Jackson McCabe; Minneapolis: Fortress Press), 233–56.

Marshall, John W. 2009. 'Gender and Empire: Sexualized Violence in John's Anti-Imperial Apocalypse', in *A Feminist Companion to the Apocalypse of John* (ed. Amy-Jill Levine with Maria Mayo Robbins; Feminist Companion to the New Testament and Early Christian Writings, 13; New York: T&T Clark), 17–32.

Martin, Clarice J. 2005. 'Polishing the Unclouded Mirror: A Womanist Reading of Revelation 18:13', in *From Every People and Nation: The Book of Revelation in Intercultural Perspective* (ed. David Rhoads; Minneapolis: Fortress Press), 82–109.

Martin, Thomas W. 2009. 'The City as Salvific Space: Heterotopic Place and Environmental Ethics in the New Jerusalem', *SBL Forum* 7.2: http://www.sbl-site.org/publications/article.aspx?ArticleId=801.

McGinn, Bernard. 2018. 'Introduction: Joachim of Fiore in the History of Western Culture', in *A Companion to Joachim of Fiore* (ed. Matthias Riedl; Brill's Companions to the Christian Tradition; Leiden, Netherlands: Brill), 1–19.

Meier, Harry O. 2002. 'There's a New World Coming! Reading the Apocalypse in the Shadow of the Canadian Rockies', in *The Earth Story in the New Testament* (ed. Norman C. Habel and Vicki Balabanski; Cleveland: The Pilgrim Press), 166–79.

Menéndez-Antuña, Luis. 2018. *Thinking Sex with the Great Whore: Deviant Sexualities and Empire in the Book of Revelation* (Routledge Interdisciplinary Perspectives on Biblical Criticism; New York: Routledge).

Míguez, Néstor. 1995. 'Apocalyptic and the Economy: A Reading of Revelation 18 from the Experience of Economic Exclusion', in *Reading from This Place: Social Location and Biblical Interpretation in Global Perspective* (ed. Fernando F. Segovia and Mary Ann Tolbert; Minneapolis: Fortress Press), 250–62.

Miller, Paul D. (2014). 'Evangelicals, Israel and US Foreign Policy', *Survival* 56: 7–26.

Moberg, Marcus. 2015. *Christian Metal: History, Ideology, Scene* (Bloomsbury Studies in Religion and Popular Music; New York: Bloomsbury Academic).

Moore, Stephen D. 2007. 'Revelation', in *A Postcolonial Commentary on the New Testament Writings* (ed. Fernando F. Segovia and R. S. Sugirtharajah; The Bible and Postcolonialism, 13; New York: T&T Clark), 436–54.

Moore, Stephen D. 2009. 'Metonymies of Empire: Sexual Humiliation and Gender Masquerade in the Book of Revelation', in *Postcolonial Interventions: Essays in Honor of R. S. Sugirtharajah* (ed. Tat-siong Benny Liew; The Bible in the Modern World, 23; Sheffield, UK: Sheffield Phoenix Press), 71–97.

Moore, Stephen D. 2014. *Untold Tales from the Book of Revelation: Sex and Gender, Empire and Ecology* (Society of Biblical Literature Resources for Biblical Study, 79; Atlanta: SBL Press).

Müntzer, Thomas. 1993. *Revelation and Revolution: Basic Writings of Thomas Müntzer* (ed. and trans. Michael G. Baylor; London and Toronto: Associated University Presses).

Nelavala, Surekha. 2009. '"Babylon the Great, Mother of Whores" (Rev. 17.5): A Postcolonial Feminist Perspective', *Expository Times* 121: 60–5.

Nicolet, Valérie, and Benoît Ischer. 2019. 'Reception of Revelation in *Darksiders*: The Case of the Four Horsemen of the Apocalypse', *Religions* 10: https://doi.org/10.3390/rel10030164.

Ogbar, Jeffrey O. G. 2004. *Black Power: Radical Politics and African American Identity* (Baltimore: Johns Hopkins University Press).

O'Hear, Natasha, and Anthony O'Hear. 2015. *Picturing the Apocalypse: The Book of Revelation in the Arts over Two Millenia* (Oxford, UK: Oxford University Press).

Økland, Jorunn. 2009. 'Why Can't the Heavenly Miss Jerusalem Just Shut Up?', in *A Feminist Companion to the Apocalypse of John* (ed. Amy Jill Levine with Maria Mayo Robbins; Feminist Companion to the New Testament and Early Christian Writings, 13; New York: T&T Clark), 88–105.

Oster, Richard E., Jr. 2013. *Seven Congregations in a Roman Crucible: A Commentary on Revelation 1–3* (Eugene, OR: Wipf and Stock).

Park, Rohun. 2008. 'Revelation for Sale: An Intercultural Reading of Revelation 18 from an East Asian Perspective', *The Bible and Theory* 4: 25.1–25.12. DOI: 10.2104/bc080025.

Parrott, Douglas M. 1990. 'Eugnostos the Blessed (III, 3 and V, 1) and the Sophia of Jesus Christ (III, 4 and BG 8502, 3)', in *The Nag Hammadi Library* (ed. James M. Robinson; rev. ed.; New York: HarperCollins), 220–43.

Partridge, Christopher, ed. 2012. *Anthems of Apocalypse: Popular Music and Apocalyptic Thought* (The Bible in the Modern World, 42; Sheffield, UK: Sheffield Phoenix Press).

Pew Research Center. 2010. 'Public Sees a Future Full of Promise and Peril. Life in 2050: Amazing Science, Familiar Threats', https://www.people-press. org/2010/06/22/public-sees-a-future-full-of-promise-and-peril/.

Pew Research Center. 2013. 'U.S. Christians' Views on the Return of Christ', https://www.pewforum.org/2013/03/26/us-christians-views-on-the-return-of-christ/.

Pieters, Albertus. 1998 [1938]. *A Candid Examination of the Scofield Bible* (Pensacola, FL: Chapel Library).

Pietsch, B. M. 2015. *Dispensational Modernism* (Oxford, UK: Oxford University Press).

Pippin, Tina. 1992. *Death and Desire: The Rhetoric of Gender in the Apocalypse of John* (Literary Currents in Biblical Interpretation; Louisville, KY: Westminster John Knox Press).

Pippin, Tina. 1995. '"And I Will Strike Her Children Dead": Death and the Deconstruction of Social Location', in *Reading from This Place*, Vol. 1: *Social Location and Biblical Interpretation in the United States* (ed. Fernando F. Segovia and Mary Ann Tolbert; Minneapolis: Fortress Press).

Pippin, Tina. 1999. *Apocalyptic Bodies: The Biblical End of the World in Text and Image* (Biblical Limits; New York: Routledge).

Pippin, Tina. 2005. 'The Heroine and the Whore: The Apocalypse of John in Feminist Perspective', in *From Every People and Nation: The Book of Revelation in Intercultural Perspective* (ed. David Rhoads; Minneapolis: Fortress Press), 127–45.

Pippin, Tina, and J. Michael Clark. 2006. 'Revelation/Apocalypse', in *The Queer Bible Commentary* (ed. Deryn Guest, Robert E. Goss, Mona West and Thomas Bohache; London: SCM Press), 753–68.

Rainbow, Jesse. 2007. 'Male *mastoi* in Revelation 1.13', *Journal for the Study of the New Testament* 30: 249–53.

Reid, Duncan. 2000. 'Setting aside the Ladder to Heaven: Revelation 21.1–22.5 from the Perspective of the Earth', in *Readings from the Perspective of Earth* (ed. Norman C. Habel; Sheffield, UK: Sheffield Academic Press), 232–45.

Richard, Pablo. 1995. *Apocalypse: A People's Commentary on the Book of Revelation* (trans. Phillip Berryman; The Bible and Liberation; Maryknoll, NY: Orbis Books).

Richard, Pablo. 2005. 'Reading the Apocalypse: Resistance, Hope, and Liberation in Central America', in *From Every People and Nation: The Book of Revelation in Intercultural Perspective* (ed. David Rhoads; Minneapolis: Fortress Press), 146–64.

Riedl, Matthias. 2016. 'Apocalyptic Violence and Revolutionary Action: Thomas Müntzer's *Sermon to the Princes*', in *A Companion to the Premodern Apocalypse* (ed. Michael A. Ryan; Brill's Companion to the Christian Tradition; Leiden, Netherlands: Brill), 260–96.

Rosen, Aaron. 2013. 'Playing the Apocalypse: Video Games and Religion', *New Humanist*, 16 October 2013: https://newhumanist.org.uk/articles/4382/playing-the-apocalypse-video-games-and-religion.

Rossing, Barbara R. 1999a. *The Choice between Two Cities: Whore, Bride, and Empire in the Apocalypse* (Harvard Theological Studies, 48; Harrisburg, PA: Trinity Press International).

Rossing, Barbara R. 1999b. 'River of Life in God's New Jerusalem: An Ecological Vision for Earth's Future', in *Christianity and Ecology* (ed. Rosemary Radford Ruether and Dieter T. Hessel; Religions of the World and Ecology, 3; Cambridge, MA: Harvard Center for World Religions), 205–24.

Rossing, Barbara R. 2002. 'Alas for Earth! Lament and Resistance in Revelation 12', in *The Earth Story in the New Testament* (ed. Norman C. Habel and Vicki Balabanski; Cleveland: The Pilgrim Press), 180–92.

Rossing, Barbara R. 2004. *The Rapture Exposed: The Message of Hope in the Book of Revelation* (New York: Basic Books).

Rossing, Barbara R. 2005. 'For the Healing of the World: Reading Revelation Ecologically', in *From Every People and Nation: The Book of Revelation in Intercultural Perspective* (ed. David Rhoads; Minneapolis: Fortress Press), 165–82.

Rossing, Barbara R. 2020. 'Lost Land: Visualizing Deforestation and Eschatology in the Apocalypse of John and the Column of Trajan in Rome', in *People and Land: Decolonizing Theologies* (ed. Jione Havea; Lanham, MD: Lexington Books/Fortress Academic), 159–74.

Ruiz, Jean-Pierre. 2003. 'Taking a Stand on the Sand of the Seashore: A Postcolonial Exploration of Revelation 13', in *Reading the Book of Revelation: A Resource for Students* (ed. David L. Barr; Atlanta: Society of Biblical Literature), 119–36.

Runions, Erin. 2014. *The Babylon Complex: Theopolitical Fantasies of War, Sex, and Sovereignty* (New York: Fordham University Press).

Sánchez, David A. 2008. *From Patmos to the Barrio: The Subversion of Imperial Myths from the Book of Revelation to the Present* (Minneapolis: Fortress Press).

Schüssler Fiorenza, Elisabeth. 1998. *The Book of Revelation: Justice and Judgment* (2nd ed.; Minneapolis: Fortress Press).

Schüssler Fiorenza, Elisabeth. 2007. *The Power of the Word: Scripture and the Rhetoric of Empire* (Minneapolis: Fortress Press).

Scofield, Cyrus I. 1917. *The Scofield Reference Bible: The Holy Bible Containing the Old and New Testaments, Authorized Version, with a New System of Connected Topical References to All the Greater Themes of Scripture, with Annotations, Revised Marginal Renderings, Summaries, Definitions, and Index, to Which Are Added Helps at Hard Places, Explanations of Seeming Discrepancies, and a New System of Paragraphs* (rev. ed.; Oxford, UK: Oxford University Press).

Selvidge, Marla J. 1996. 'Reflections on Violence and Pornography: Misogyny in the Apocalypse and Ancient Hebrew Prophecy', in *A Feminist Companion to the Hebrew Bible in the New Testament* (ed. Athalya Brenner; The Feminist Companion to the Bible, 10; Sheffield, UK: Sheffield Academic Press), 274–85.

Sintado, Carlos Alberto. 2015. *Social Ecology, Ecojustice, and the New Testament: Liberating Readings* (Geneva, Switzerland: Globalethics.net).

Slater, Thomas B. 1999. *Christ and Community: A Socio-Historical Study of the Christology of Revelation* (Journal for the Study of the New Testament Supplement Series, 178; Sheffield, UK: Sheffield Academic Press).

Smith, Shanell T. 2014. *The Woman Babylon and the Marks of Empire: Reading Revelation with a Postcolonial Womanist Hermeneutics of Ambiveilence* (Emerging Scholars; Minneapolis: Fortress Press).

Stenström, Hanna. 2009. '"They Have Not Defiled Themselves with Women …": Christian Identity According to the Book of Revelation', in *A Feminist Companion to the Apocalypse of John* (ed. Amy-Jill Levine with Maria Mayo Robbins; Feminist Companion to the New Testament and Early Christian Writings, 13; New York: T&T Clark), 33–54.

Swete, Henry Barclay. 1906. *The Apocalypse of St. John: The Greek Text with Introduction, Notes and Indices* (London: Macmillan).

Tabbernee, William, and Peter Lampe. 2008. *Pepouza and Tymion: The Discovery and Archaeological Exploration of an Ancient City and an Imperial Estate* (Berlin: Walter de Gruyter).

Thomas, Eric A. 2018. 'The Futures Outside: Apocalyptic Epilogue Unveiled as Africana Queer Prologue', in *Sexual Disorientations: Queer Temporalities, Affects, Theologies* (ed. Kent L. Brintnall, Joseph A. Marchal, and Stephen D. Moore; Transdisciplinary Theological Colloquia; New York: Fordham University Press), 90–112.

Thomas, Rodney Lawrence. 2010. *Magical Motifs in the Book of Revelation* (Library of New Testament Studies; New York: T&T Clark).

Till, Rupert. 2012. 'Metal and the Beast: The Adoption of Apocalyptic Imagery in Heavy Metal Music', in *Anthems of Apocalypse: Popular Music and Apocalyptic Thought* (ed. Christopher Partridge; The Bible in the Modern World, 42; Sheffield, UK: Sheffield Phoenix Press), 90–108.

Vander Stichele, Caroline. 2000. 'Just a Whore: The Annihilation of Babylon According to Revelation 17.16', *Lectio Difficilior* 1: http://www.lectio.unibe.ch/00_1/j.htm.

Vander Stichele, Caroline. 2009. 'Re-membering the Whore: The Fate of Babylon According to Revelation 17.16', in *A Feminist Companion to the Apocalypse of John* (ed. Amy-Jill Levine with Maria Mayo Robbins; Feminist Companion to the New Testament and Early Christian Writings, 13; New York: T&T Clark), 106–20.

Wagner, Rachel. 2015. 'Video Games and Religion', *Oxford Handbooks Online*, September 2015: https://doi.10.1093/oxfordhb/9780199935420.013.8.

Wainwright, Arthur W. 2001. *Mysterious Apocalypse: Interpreting the Book of Revelation* (Eugene, OR: Wipf and Stock).

Walker, Alice. 1982. *The Color Purple* (New York: Mariner Books).

Walliss, John, and Lee Quinby, eds. 2010. *Reel Revelations: Apocalypse and Film* (The Bible in the Modern World, 31; Sheffield, UK: Sheffield Phoenix Press).

Yarbro Collins, Adela. 1996. *Cosmology and Eschatology in Jewish and Christian Apocalypticism* (Supplements to the Journal for the Study of Judaism, 50; Leiden, Netherlands: Brill).

Yarbro Collins, Adela. 2001. *The Combat Myth in the Book of Revelation* (Eugene, OR: Wipf and Stock).

Index of Biblical References

Index of Authors

www.ingramcontent.com/pod-product-compliance
Ingram Content Group UK Ltd.
Pitfield, Milton Keynes, MK11 3LW, UK
UKHW020703280225
455688UK00004B/232